Living the Magnificat

Sweet is the scene where genial friendship plays

The pleasing game of interchanging praise.

Oliver Wendell Holmes 1809-94

Dennis remembering
Summer 2007

Living the Magnificat

Affirming Catholicism in a Broken World

Edited by

Mark D. Chapman

mowbray

Published by Mowbray
A Continuum Imprint
The Tower Building
11 York Road
London SE1 7NX

80 Maiden Lane, Suite 704
New York
NY 10038

www.continuumbooks.com

First published 2007

British Library Cataloguing-in-Publication Data
A catalogue record for this book is available from the British Library

Typeset by the author
Printed and bound in Great Britain by Athenaeum Press Ltd,
Gateshead, Tyne and Wear

ISBN 10: 1–9062-8606-X (paperback)
ISBN 13: 978–1-9062–8606-4 (paperback)

Contents

Acknowledgements

Thanks are due to the Revd Richard Jenkins, and Lisa Martell, Director and Administrator of Affirming Catholicism, and to Liz Badman and the planning group, for their energy and commitment in organising the conference 'Living the Magnificat: God's Cry for Justice, Mercy and Humility' where these chapters were first delivered as lectures. I am also grateful to the Very Revd Jeffrey John for providing a foreword. Once again we benefited greatly from the hospitality of the staff of St Chad's College, Durham, as well as the efficiency of the conference manager James Randle and his youthful assistants. They helped make the conference such a happy occasion. Indeed without them there would have been no conference and no book. St Chad's is a marvellous place for Christians to gather together, and the neighbouring cathedral adds a certain something to the ambience of holiness.

Notes on Contributors

James Alison is a Roman Catholic theologian, priest, and author. Having lived with the Dominican Order between 1981 and 1995, he currently travels the world as an itinerant preacher, lecturer, and retreat giver. His most recent book is *Undergoing God: Dispatches From the Scene of a Break-in* (DLT).

Joseph P. Cassidy is Principal of St Chad's College, Durham. Originally from Canada he spent thirteen years as a Jesuit. His research interests focus on the place of the heart in ethics.

Stephen Cottrell is Bishop of Reading in the Diocese of Oxford. Before that he was Diocesan Missioner in Wakefield, Springboard Missioner and Canon Pastor of Peterborough Cathedral. He is the author of many books on mission. His most recent book is *From the Abundance of the Heart: Catholic Evangelism for All Christians* (DLT).

Mark D. Chapman is vice-principal of Ripon College Cuddesdon and has published widely in the fields of Church History and many other aspects of theology. His most recent books are *Anglicanism: A Very Short Introduction* (OUP) and *Bishops, Saints and Politics* (T & T Clark). He is publications officer for Affirming Catholicism.

Michael Doe Michael Doe is General Secretary of what is now USPG: Anglicans in World Mission, having previously served as the first Bishop of Swindon in the Diocese of Bristol. After the 1998 Lambeth Conference he wrote *Seeking the Truth in Love: The Church and Homosexuality* (DLT).

Mongezi Guma is currently chairperson of the South African Government Commission for the Rights of Cultural, Religious and Linguistic Communities. Before that he was Director of the Ecumenical Service for Socio-Economic Transformation. He is also Rector of the church of Christ the King, Sophiatown.

Linda Hogan is head of the Irish School of Ecumenics, Dublin and Professor at Trinity College. She is author of a number of books on women's spirituality and ethics, including *Confronting the Truth: Conscience in the Catholic Tradition* (DLT).

Jeffrey John is Dean of St Albans and was previously Canon Theologian of Southwark Cathedral. He was a founder member of Affirming Catholicism.

Sr Margaret Magdalen CSMV is a member of the Community of St Mary the Virgin, Wantage. She has worked in Botswana and most recently in Sheffield.

Foreword

MOTHER of God! no lady thou:
Common woman of common earth;
'Our Lady' ladies call thee now,
But Christ was never of gentle birth;
A common man of the common earth.

For God's ways are not as our ways:
The noblest lady in the land
Would have given up half her days,
Would have cut off her right hand,
To bear the child that was God of the land.

Never a lady did He choose,
Only a maid of low degree,
So humble she might not refuse
The carpenter of Galilee:
A daughter of the people, she.

Mary Elizabeth Coleridge in her poem 'Our Lady'
presents Mary as a revolutionary figure whose power is
not to be tamed by sugary pieties. Writing long before the
Liberation Theologians but very much in their spirit, she was
insisting on a long-neglected truth of the Gospel. Most of what
we hear about Mary comes from Luke, and Luke is very clear
that Mary represents the *anawim*, the humble people of Israel:
the underclass, the losers and the victims. Above all her
Magnificat, framed around the song of Hannah from 1 Samuel
2, consists almost entirely of quotations from Old Testament
passages about the poor. Mary's song is their song: she is the

voice of the voiceless whom God at last has heard and is going to vindicate, because he is going to turn the old order upside down.

When Mary is heard and understood in this way, she becomes a dangerous figure for the rich, powerful or oppressive. In the 1980s the dictatorship of Guatemala actually forbade the public reading of the Magnificat as an incitement to rebellion and a danger to the state. If that surprises us, it is only because we are so used to hearing or reciting it as a matter of ritual habit that we no longer notice how subversive it is.

Mary represents not only the economically poor and struggling; she represents the socially despised and rejected as well. As far as the world was concerned, Mary was an unmarried mother and Jesus her illegitimate son (as the Pharisees sarcastically remind him in John 8.41). It is still hard enough to be an unmarried mother today in our own society; the stigma in first-century Palestine was a great deal worse. But this was part of what Mary's acceptance of God's plan for her entailed. From the first Jesus and Mary were marked by a struggle with rejecting, hostile forces which they had to bear together. As she followed him through the trials and joys of his earthly ministry, she 'stored them up in her heart'; and in the end, as she stood at the foot of the cross, Simeon's prophecy that 'the sword would also pierce' her own heart proved fully true. That is why she is such a source of hope and consolation for so many people in so many different situations of struggle. Her experience reflects the struggles of all who try to live by the Spirit of her Son against the world's enmity.

But if Mary and her Magnificat challenge the world and its values, they also challenge the Church no less powerfully. In scripture and in tradition there is a strong symbolic link – sometimes it seems almost an identity – between Mary and the Church. From the Cross Jesus gives Mary to be mother of St John, and by extension – so tradition has taught from very early days – mother of all Jesus' beloved disciples. In the extraordinary vision of the Glorified Woman in Revelation 12, Mary must clearly be the historical basis of the picture since the woman portrayed is the one who gives birth to the Saviour. Yet at the same time Mary is overlaid with a wealth of mystical imagery that presents her as the new and redeemed Israel, a prefiguring of the Church in glory (just as in the Magnificat she is presented as the ultimate daughter of Zion, a type of all that was best in the old Israel). The vision of Revelation 12 is, as it were, a vision of the promise of the Magnificat realised – Mary, the representative of the lowest of the low, has now been raised by God to the highest height to share in his glory, crowned with the sun and with the moon at the her feet – although her offspring 'who keep the commandments of God and bear testimony to Jesus' still have to wage war against the forces of evil on earth.

Mary symbolises the Church in its perfection. But the dangers of making a too swift, too easy identification between Mary and Church are obvious. Mary glorified is still the same Mary of Nazareth, the peasant girl who suffered with her Son and followed in his way. She is not a goddess. The Church forgets at its peril that Mary is glorified only *because* of her poverty, *because* she followed God's call, *because* she represents and furthers the hopes of the *anawim*. Where the Church rests too readily in its own power and glory; where it sets its own institutional life and survival above its solidarity with the poor and rejected; where it allies itself with the forces of oppression, prejudice and contempt; or worse, where it becomes itself the persecutor and the oppressor – then the identification with Mary is lost. And if the Church is no longer the Church of Mary and the Magnificat, it is no longer the Church of Christ.

The great virtue of this book is that it presents us with a sharp challenge to our churchy as well as to our worldly assumptions, and reminds us what Mary's uncompromising song really means. It forces us to ask the question: who exactly are the rich and powerful now, and who are the *anawim*, the humble and meek? And we – corporately and individually – which ones are we, and whose side are we really on?

> Out she sang the song of her heart.
> Never a lady so had sung.
> She knew no letters, had no art;
> To all mankind, in woman's tongue,
> Hath Israelitish Mary sung.
>
> And still for men to come she sings,
> Nor shall her singing pass away.
> 'He hath filled the hungry with good things' –
> O listen, lords and ladies gay! –
> 'And the rich He hath sent empty away.'

JEFFREY JOHN
St Albans
The Feast of the Visitation of the
Blessed Virgin Mary to Elizabeth
2007

Introduction:
Living the Magnificat

MARK D. CHAPMAN

The chapters collected in this book were originally given as lectures and sermons at the September 2006 Affirming Catholicism Conference which was once again held in the congenial surroundings of St Chad's College, Durham and its neighbouring and awe-inspiring cathedral. The theme of the conference was 'Living the Magnificat: God's Cry for Justice, Mercy and Humility', which was addressed explicitly by most of the papers. Since all of the earlier conferences of Affirming Catholicism had been on 'religious' themes (although many contained significant and ethical reflection), it seemed to the organisers that perhaps Affirming Catholics had been seduced by the idea that when church people gather together they ought to be talking about religious or spiritual things. But, of course, Christ came to save the world and not the Church – in an Anglican Communion which at the time of the conference was looking ever more inwardly at itself and which was pre-occupied with its own crisis of identity, it seemed crucial to look outwards, towards the suffering world. To look outwards seemed particularly important, especially as Anglo-Catholics have a long and distinguished history of engagement with politics and the transformation of the world, both in the United Kingdom and elsewhere. This can easily be forgotten in our constant obsession with church life and order.

So we turned to the great biblical themes of justice and mercy, but not in a spirit of triumphalism or complacency: that always seems inappropriate in the church. Both of these great virtues have so often been overlooked by a discriminatory and

1

judgmental institution which has sometimes been last to embrace equality, where it has embraced it at all. Instead we sought to approach the world with a humility that comes with listening out for God's voice amid the often contradictory and competing voices of our world and church. In planning the conference we arrived at a number of guiding questions: what is it that really matters for Christians? How is God's will to be discerned as we try to live our lives today? How should Christians participate in the messy world of politics?

The different speakers addressed these questions in very different ways, but what brings the essays and sermons together is a common search to find contemporary meaning in the Magnificat – in that great song of praise uttered by God's humble and lowly servant, Mary, Mother of God and Mother of the Church. Those great words, which are so often sung at Evensong in the beautiful architectural setting of an English cathedral and with the exquisite musical performance of a professional choir, became the *leitmotif* of the conference. But the aesthetics of Anglicanism can easily dull the sense of the words. To praise and magnify God, and to put God before everything else, as Mary does in her song, leads on to a revolutionary political agenda where the lowly are exalted and the proud are scattered in the imagination of their hearts. Justice will triumph through praise, through the re-orientation of our priorities; and it was precisely that agenda that motivated her Son as he fought the authorities of his own world.

One of the great tragedies of the European Reformation is that Mary was so often associated with some of the excesses of the medieval church that her central role in salvation was often overlooked. Despite being the most popular patron of English parish churches, the figure of Mary has not loomed large in mainstream Anglican religious life for many hundreds of years. Lady Day, the Feast of the Annunciation, marked the start of the New Year and was the day on which agricultural rents were due, but it ceased to be observed with religious devotion. Although the Prayer Book calendar also includes the Purification (Candlemas), the Visitation, the Nativity, and the Conception, these were hardly major feasts of the church. But Mary, who features so prominently in Western art through the whole of the Middle Ages, is central to the Christian faith – she is the one on whom Christ's flesh depended; she is the one who nurtured him in her womb, and who educated him through his childhood. She was the first disciple as she accepted God's call. Mary trusted God in humility – and through that trust the world was re-created. But something else is also true about Mary, and it is perhaps far more shocking – Mary wasn't the only obedient and humble agent. The other side of the same act is that God in his own humility and obedience trusted Mary as well. It seems to me that this aspect of Mary's role is central for the whole understanding of human salvation.

Nurturing, educating and letting-go

Let me explain what I mean by thinking through the scenes of Mary's life. First comes the Annunciation. The good news that she is to bear Christ is greeted with fear and with incredulity: 'how can this be, for I am still a virgin?' (Lk. 1.34). But Mary accepts her destiny; she is the one in whom creation is to be restored. But, of course, from where we stand we can never know whether she had a say in the matter. We can never know whether any doubts went through her mind, even for an instant, before she replied to the angel. And we can never know whether her 'so be it', her 'be it unto me according to thy word' (Lk. 1.38), was a considered, a thought out, response, or whether it was forced upon her by the Most High.

Although we're not told, it seems to me that it is unlikely that Mary had much say in the matter – after all she calls herself the Lord's servant, and that means literally the Lord's female slave (δούλη κυρίου). God's dealings with Mary seem to be very much a one-sided transaction: the Lord tells his slave what to do, and the slave does what she is told – and like an obedient slave she has no real choice in the matter.

Throughout Christian history the story of Mary has often been read as the story of obedience – the story of obedience to the commands of God. She is the counterpart to the disobedient Eve and reverses the consequences of the Fall. In some art she is depicted as trampling on the serpent. And because of this she is elevated into the archetype for all human beings, but especially women. Obedience and service become the lot of the human being in observance of the will of God, a will so frequently interpreted by the men who serve in the offices of the church. We may well suppose that Mary might have preferred somebody else to have been overshadowed by the Most High God, but whatever her feelings she couldn't do anything about it. God chose and Mary obeyed.

But there is more to Mary than simple obedience. After all, we need to ask: what sort of obedience is it when we don't really have any choice in the matter? What sort of contract is it when one party is the Lord and other is his lowly female slave? This may not strike us as very fair. And it would suggest that Mary's 'Be it unto me according to thy word' means nothing more than this: just do whatever you want and I shall obey. And if we use this as an example of earthly obedience then it can soon become very dangerous: after all, 'I was only obeying orders' is a frequently pleaded excuse. Similarly, the response, 'Do whatever you want with me and I shall obey', is hardly the recipe for a good marriage. It is one of the great tragedies in the history of the church that the example of Mary's obedience has been used to justify the misuse and even abuse of power, especially between men and women. This is hardly surprising given that so many of our images of God are of power, majesty, and sovereignty – the king with orb and sceptre in his

4

hands;[1] or the mighty warrior in battle, slaying his enemies.[2] Such a God is the powerful God who subdues his slaves, who overwhelms his servants, and who commands total obedience. Against such a God Mary has very little say in what she does.

But, it seems to me, the contract is not quite so one-sided. If we move from the Annunciation to the Visitation, then we can begin to say something more about Mary's act of obedience. After she has declared that she will obey God, Mary goes on to visit her relative, Elizabeth, who is also miraculously pregnant with John the Baptist.[3] I think it is the sheer fact of pregnancy that offers us another perspective about Mary's great act of obedience. Mary is now nurturing Jesus in her womb and that means that God is now dependent on her. The powerful one, the Most High who overshadowed her and who seemed to leave her no say in the matter, is now in her womb. God has entrusted himself to her body. And that means that God himself in the person of his Son is now totally helpless – just like any other child in any womb. He is totally powerless; totally at the mercy of his mother and he shares all the risks of a first-century pregnancy. Here there is a strange reversal of the order of the world; God himself is dethroned. The master has made himself dependent on his young girl slave. And for many that may not seem like the proper way for an all-powerful God to behave.

Moving on to the next chapter of Luke and to the story of Christmas there is again something more to be said about the role of Mary. God is born of this lowly slave girl in the same way as all the rest of us. We can easily forget this, especially as we often speak of the Virgin Birth, when what we mean is a virginal conception. There was nothing virginal about the birth itself; it was as painful and as difficult and as dangerous as any

---

1   See, for instance, Heb. 1.8.

2   See, for instance, Zeph. 3.17.

3   Lk. 1.39–56.

other birth at the time. There was certainly no epidural, or even gas and air, in the stable. Who knows whether there was even a midwife? And, of course, this risk-taking continued through infancy. God's power is revealed in the sheer helplessness of the baby who relies for everything on its mother; the baby Jesus suckles at her breast. This means that Christ, the very expression of God's power, is totally and utterly dependent on Mary his mother; on her blood supply; on the food she eats and drinks. Without Mary there would be no Christ. That is a commitment to let Mary be; that is an act of extreme trust on the part of God: he has chosen not to be master, not to be powerful, but to hang on a mother's breast in total dependency.

Jesus doesn't come into the world as some divine emissary putting everything to rights. He wasn't transplanted on earth like some alien endowed with supernatural powers – that is what is wrong with the apocryphal Gospels with their strange stories of the infant Jesus performing wonderful deeds. Instead Jesus comes in the most ordinary of ways. And for the rest of his childhood we can assume that there is nothing extraordinary about Jesus – he develops like other children; he grows and he learns. From the total dependence of the baby he takes the first leaps into independence – and he does that in the very ordinary world of a carpenter's shop at Nazareth. There is no festal glory there, just the noisy work of human labour.

This forgotten time when Jesus grows up is one of the most tantalising times of all – it is that period when Jesus has to learn and to grow up like the rest of us. He has to explore what it means to be a person, to be an individual thinking for himself. We can imagine ourselves into the house at Nazareth and we can think of a little boy playing with his toys and doing all those things little boys do, occupying his time with the first-century equivalents of Lego; but also presumably doing things that he should not have done as well – and having to be told off. After all, he would not have been a human being, let alone a little boy, without the occasional misdemeanour. And that does not compromise Christ's sinlessness: all of us have to learn how to be human before we can be sinners.

The Holy House at Nazareth was not like Walsingham or Loreto, full of pilgrims and candles and altars; instead it was a real house of real people doing real things. And it is in this house that Jesus learns right from wrong. Without Mary, without Joseph, he would never have known how to be human. I am not usually overly excited by Pre-Raphaelite art, which can be excessively sentimental, but Millais' famous picture in the Tate Gallery of *Christ in the House of His Parents* (also known as *The Carpenter's Shop*) of 1849–50 captures the scene well. Christ stands between his mother and his earthly father apparently being given wisdom by both. It is almost as if Joseph is anointing Christ with his worldly knowledge in a strange reversal of the annunciation.

We have rather sanitised our pictures of Jesus' upbringing – everyone has seen the great Renaissance pictures of Mary dressed in a beautiful gown with a plump Italianate baby on her lap, both of them radiating haloes. But there is another rather more recent image that is far more striking. In 1926 the great surrealist painter Max Ernst painted Mary with Jesus laid across her lap – it is called *The Holy Virgin Punishes the Christ Child in the Presence of Three Witnesses: A. B., P. E., and Artist.* She is chastising him with some vigour with three surrealist observers watching through the window. The scene was shocking at the time and eventually led to Max Ernst's public excommunication by the Archbishop of Cologne. Whatever the rights and wrongs of corporal punishment, what is most striking about the picture is its emphasis on God's humanity – on Jesus learning right from wrong, learning how to be a human being from his mother. Jesus had to be educated – he had to mature and grow and he had to learn like the rest us: reading, writing, and arithmetic. He had to enter into that network of relationships we call society, to learn its rules, its structures and its organisation: and in the first century that no doubt involved some rather physical forms of discipline.

But gradually there is a moving on. Jesus has to remove himself from the comforts of childhood to become a fully-fledged adult. And for this to happen there has to be a letting-go by Mary and Joseph – another act of trust shared by every other parent. It is easy to sympathize with Mary and Joseph when they find Jesus in the Temple at the age of twelve. Mary says to him: 'Son, why have you treated us so? Behold your father and I have been looking for you anxiously.'[4] Like any other child Jesus causes worries for his parents. But again like any other human being he has to work out boundaries and priorities and relationships. There is another wonderful picture that illustrates this beautifully. In Simone Martini's luxurious painting of this scene in the Walker Art Gallery in Liverpool, painted in about 1342, Joseph is pleading with Jesus, and Mary is pointing her hand in anxiety. And Christ appears with his hands crossed – no doubt intended as a sign of the passion which is to come, but also the sign of the stroppy teenager resisting parental authority. Nurturing, educating and letting-go – all these are signs of God's humanity revealed through Mary.

Human maturing is a difficult process – it implies a relation of trust which can so often be shocking and frightening. The future is unknown. And of course for Mary there are portents of what is to happen. After the story of the Presentation in the Temple when Mary is re-introduced into the Community, the Old Simeon speaks to Mary. 'This child,' he says – the helpless baby in her arms – 'is destined to be a sign that will be opposed', and her own heart will be pierced.[5] As that child matures so he will be rejected by those who cannot accept him. The great risk for Mary was in letting her son go – but without

---

4   Lk. 2.48.
5   Lk. 2.35.

that risk there would have been no Gospel, and God would not have been the God we know in Jesus Christ.

And ultimately this leads on to the picture of Mary at the foot of the cross, looking on, unable to comprehend: the son she loved is dying. But the sword that pierces her soul is the sword that was first unsheathed in the humble family at Nazareth: Jesus had to learn to be human before he could shock and disturb the world. Jesus trusted that world and the world condemned him as an outlaw; it refused to respond to that trust. And that led to the cross – to the pushing out of God from the protective nurturing of his servants.

The logic of all this is obvious. Christian understandings of power, trust, commitment, embodiment, and justice all flow from God's simple act of obedience to Mary. A new form of relationship between God and the world is displayed, based not on power but on love – on God's utter commitment to Mary and to every other human being. And it is from this commitment to all of us, from the reversal of values so eloquently voiced in the Magnificat, that we can begin to hear God's cry for justice, mercy and humility. The world matters because that is where God chose to live his life, and God trusts us to do the same.

Living the Magnificat

Mary is approached in this volume from a number of different perspectives – but all of the contributions assume something of the direct relationship between the incarnation understood through the role of Mary, and the transformation of the world expressed in the Magnificat. In his sparkling and thought-provoking essay, for instance, James Alison describes her role in the recreation of the world, using an extended, original, and suggestive operatic analogy. Similarly, in her extended discussion of the nature of globalisation, the Irish Roman

Catholic theologian, Linda Hogan, offers challenges to the Church as it seeks to rise to the new problems presented by the global age. The South African theologian, Mongezi Guma, sees Mary as giving voice to the voiceless, and as an example to be followed in the work of reconciliation between hitherto estranged people. Stephen Cottrell sees Mary as placing God literally in the centre of her life, which has earth-shattering consequences. My own chapter moves in a slightly different direction – it is less concerned with Mary, and more to do with the need for openness in both the church and the world. My anxiety is that it is very easy for all Christians, including Affirming Catholics, to be seduced by the finite and tightly defined boundaries of a church party. The Christian contribution to politics, I suggest, ought to be based on a humility and an open-endedness which should make Christians thorns in the flesh of all political leaders.

The three other contributions to this volume are concerned with learning to live with difference and to be open to transformation through encounter with one another, especially with those very different from ourselves. The two sermons in the volume both offer insights in dealing with difference. Drawing on her experience in Botswana, Sr Margaret Magdalen CSMV suggests that the real Christian ethic is one of hospitality and acceptance which can transform both parties in an encounter. Joseph Cassidy challenges the reader to think through the nature of Christian moral universalism, suggesting the possibility of ethical transformation through learning from the outsider. Michael Doe describes his experience of the Anglican Communion as General Secretary of USPG, offering a more optimistic view of what is happening across the world than is often presented, but also suggesting that there needs to be a refocusing on what really matters – the values of the Magnificat.

This book is offered to stimulate thinking and to help readers engage with the complex world in which they find themselves.

It does not offer simple answers or ready-made solutions. Instead it seeks to redirect our attention to the world beyond the church through the witness of the most important woman in the whole of human history, Mary, the slave girl from Nazareth. Her revolutionary words mark a fitting conclusion to this Introduction:

> And Mary said, 'My soul magnifies the Lord,
> and my spirit rejoices in God my Saviour,
> for he has looked with favour
> on the lowliness of his servant.
> Surely, from now on all generations will call me blessed;
> for the Mighty One has done great things for me,
> and holy is his name.
> His mercy is for those who fear him
> from generation to generation.
> He has shown strength with his arm;
> he has scattered the proud in the thoughts of their hearts.
> He has brought down the powerful from their thrones,
> and lifted up the lowly;
> he has filled the hungry with good things,
> and sent the rich away empty.
> He has helped his servant Israel,
> in remembrance of his mercy,
> according to the promise he made to our ancestors,
> to Abraham and to his descendants forever.'[6]

---

6   Lk. 1.46–55 (NRSV).

1

Living the Magnificat with Rossini and Mary

JAMES ALISON

I am going to be slightly naughty in this chapter. The evening on which it is being delivered is the first Vespers of the Feast of the Birthday of Our Lady. For this reason I thought that I would take advantage of the fact that although the principal theme of the conference is to look at ethical matters – as is indicated by the conference's subtitle: 'God's Cry for Justice, Mercy and Humility' – this is to be approached through the words of Our Lady. Now ethics without grace tends to moralism; and the shape, the pattern, of grace which informs ethics is a far subtler matter, and one much more difficult to pin down, than we usually attend to. So to put the whole of the conference into a theological context I am going to try to offer something in the way of prefatory remarks about the shape of grace which is revealed to us through the presence of Our Lady.

Over the last few years I have been giving, in different places, an adult catechesis course, a sort of introduction to the Christian faith. As time has gone by, I have become increasingly aware of how much more important the presence of Our Lady is in the life of faith and the life of the Church than I had hitherto thought and than seems to be current in many quarters. By this I mean her presence not as an add-on extra, or a nice metaphor for talking about the Church corporately, or an obligatory piece of fusty piety, but as a currently active player in the lived-out drama of salvation in whose midst we come to be Church. And she is a currently active player with a far larger and more sophisticated role than has been allowed in these British Isles for several hundred years. She is one to whom we have direct access; one to whom we can talk; and from whom we can receive abundantly. In other words, I want to suggest as part of my introduction to the faith that if in our enthusiasm and delight for having been invited into, and being encouraged to play around within, this extraordinarily safe drama which is Christianity we are *not* assumed to be idolaters when it comes to Our Lady, then there may well be something wrong with the way we are receiving and living the Catholic faith.

Performing Rossini

Let me spin out with you an analogy which, I hope, despite its inexactitude, will make the point. My friends know to their cost that I am a member of that small but completely mad group of devotees known as 'Rossini-nuts'. For some reason the music of the genius of Pesaro gets to us, fills our souls, and cartwheels around with delight in us in a way that no other music does. Well, for the sake of this analogy, please assume that Rossini is God; and that you are attending the opera, *The Barber of Seville*, because performances of *Mathilde di Shabran* are so hard to come by. (It does not really matter which opera: you are attending God's creation). In this performance of the *Barber*, the role of Rosina will be sung by a stunning soprano whom we will call Maria. Now the moment the music starts, Rossini is everywhere, permeating everything, his music filling out the spaces and the interstices with creative energy and beat. But Rossini is not visible: it is the music which gives him away, and the music which envelopes you. As the opera develops, different characters come on, among them Rosina. In a really good performance, it will seem as though the music that she sings is coming through Maria, that she really is incarnating the person whom the music conjures up. That is: the more herself she really is, the more irrepressible and bubbly and daring and fun and intelligent, the more Rossini's music will have done what it was intended to do.

And when it gets to the end of the opera, the audience will likely go quite mad about her, whooping and cheering and stomping. Now imagine some dour commentator saying 'That's all wrong. They should have been whooping and cheering for Rossini, not for her. In fact, by adoring her in this way, they were undercutting the praise they owed to the composer.' I hope that the excited public would have had the good sense to reply: 'But this is nonsense: what she did was what Rossini made, and every praise of her falls on him. Rossini's music wouldn't have been better if she had kept silent during all the bits when her character sings, so that we only heard Rossini. In fact it was only because she was so exultantly performing Rossini that we heard what Rossini was really about at all. Her performance was Rossini made three-dimensional and fulfilling its creative possibilities.'

Well, this, as I understand it, is what is meant by the first line of the Magnificat: 'My soul magnifies the Lord.' It means exactly what it says: God is made bigger, magnified, by Our Lady's soul. The lived-out shape of her bodily life over time is actually going to make God to be more God than before, in just the same way, I would suggest, as a really superlative operatic heroine will make Rossini be more Rossini than he was before her performance. And Rossini would have been delighted to be made more than he was before by the heroine: that was why he was busy providing the raw material from which the heroine created the role. So we can imagine God delighting in being made spontaneously great in the life of Our Lady. And we can perhaps also imagine the sadness of the angels at those who feel that God's being more is somehow threatened by the really superlative performance of someone who is in no way at all in rivalry with God.

The second line of the Magnificat helps to fill out something about the shape of the role which Our Lady is performing. Her spirit whoops (ἠγαλλίασεν) for joy at God her saviour. And this comes from a word (ἀγαλλιάω) which comes into Greek from biblical sources, and which really does have that unkempt, unbound quality of exultation which it is the peculiar genius of we northern peoples to have excluded from the serious adult business known as religion. But this is something I would like to emphasise. The presence of Our Lady in the household of faith is hugely tied up with joy, with rejoicing, with bubbling over. Just think how many of the anthems corresponding to Our Lady begin '*Gaude!*' – 'Rejoice!' And think how her feasts are all occasions of joy. How tawdry it is that in this country we have an August Bank Holiday rather than a holiday for the Assumption of Our Lady. And how impoverished is our understanding of what we have been given when Marian rejoicing is not allowed to pulsate as the constant backdrop to our faith.

So what I would like to do with you now is to begin to develop my operatic image in such a way as to make it more three-dimensional – for there is something rather special about the particular performance of *The Barber of Seville* which we are discussing. For in this performance, Rossini, not content with providing the music and thus being everywhere in the opera, is actually performing the role of the Count of Almaviva himself. Thus, in addition to being everywhere, he is also going to be present in a strictly limited sense. Gioachino is coming on stage to sing the very demanding tenor role in person. (As an historical note, I should indicate that Rossini did indeed have a tenor voice, and occasionally used it to sing in public performance. That he appears to have had a higher sense of its musical worth than did his contemporaries is something in which we unacknowledged heroes or heroines of the operatic shower cubicle can take delight).

So Rossini is everywhere, as indicated by the music, and he is present in a quite particular sense in the role of the Count of Almaviva. Surely this will give comfort to our dour commentators! Now they can mutter that Maria, singing Rosina, shouldn't really be given more than tepid applause, while all the applause at the end should go to Rossini, both for his immediate presence in singing Almaviva and for his background presence in having written the whole opera. Again, I hope you would see that this is nonsense. For Rossini to have been a great Almaviva will have required a performance of the whole opera in which the role of Almaviva interacted with the other characters. Almaviva will have helped suggest the character of Rosina into being by singing with her or against her as the scene determines, but producing a tension and that sense of artists sparking off from each other, and becoming more than themselves, which is the characteristic of a truly great performance. And, of course, it is not only Almaviva who would have sparked off Rosina but the other way round as well: a Rosina who is on fire in her role will nudge a performing Almaviva into producing a yet more dazzling account of his role. And the public will go nuts at the end in the degree of the affection they have for, and the enjoyment they have received from, each of the characters. But it will certainly not occur to them to think that they should dampen their enthusiasm for the other characters merely because Rossini was on stage rather than in the conductor's box, or behind the scenes.

Well, so far, so obvious. There is in principle nothing about praising a creature which diminishes the honour due to the creator when the creature is being praised for her particular excellence in her living out her creatureliness. And when, as in the Incarnation of our Lord and Saviour, the Creator chooses to act out the role of principal protagonist in a drama set entirely within the bounds of creatureliness, the role of the interacting creatures is made not more opaque but, at least potentially, more magnificent. The presence of the composer as character on stage does not upstage his fellow performers, but rather adds brilliance to them.

Let me now move even further into my bizarre Rossini heresy (not to be confused with the recently rehabilitated 'errors' of Rosmini). This is the moment when we finally move from the theatre into life – to where Rossini instead of being merely a theatrical composer becomes God everywhere. And where we, instead of being mere spectators at a theatrical performance, turn out to be people invited into becoming live participants in the definitive creation of the definitive masterwork called not opera, but '*Opus Dei*' (with apologies to those who are seeking to patent the whole performance for their group). What this means is that as we accept the invitation, so we find ourselves increasingly interacting with the members of the original cast as we take the show live, and as we engage in a creative multiplying effect. Because of this it is worthwhile thinking a little about our relationship to some of those original cast members.

Of course, Rossini singing the role of the Count was unforgettable, and, of course, his performance is likely to be definitive, meaning that it is something that all subsequent lyric tenors who would undertake the role must study to see how it should be done. But it was not definitive in the sense that no one else could ever sing the role again because they wouldn't be Rossini. On the contrary, it was definitive in the sense that it set out the parameters which made it possible for many other people to be Rossini. Or, as Someone Else said:

> Truly, truly, I say to you, he who believes in me will also do the works that I do; and greater works than these will he do, because I go to the Father. Whatever you ask in my name, I will do it, that the Father may

be glorified in the Son; if you ask anything in my name, I will do it.[1]

Again, as an historical aside, Rossini was not at all a control freak in his music: he used to listen to the singers he had to hand first and then actually wrote the arias for them in order to show off their voices to their best advantage. His music consequently gives singers plenty of chance to run around doing their own thing. Rossini would have been the first to recognise that there are different qualities of tenor voice than the one his physiognomy gifted him with, and that each should see what he could make of the role starting with what he had. Empowering others for flexible imitation is the underlying dynamic of this performance – just as it is of the performance whose Protagonist is the Incarnate Word.

And of course we are all familiar with the way in which we should learn to perform the role of Rosina in flexible imitation of the way that Maria first sang it. In fact, we tend to get rather too many sententious reminders that Maria's role is the same as ours, that we too should give our consent to the Angel and bring forth the Word into the world. On the one hand, we tend to insist on the unique and sacred nature of the performance carried out for us by the composer when he came onto the scene as protagonist, in a way that obscures the sense of his performing the role so as to make it possible for us to create more wonderful and freer performances. And on the other hand, we have in recent years been taught to insist on the non-unique and non-sacred nature of the leading lady's role, and how all the really important bits about her role are the ones which we do anyhow, so we don't really need to interact with her at all. Because of that we tend to downplay the bits of her role which she was the first to do, which she created under

---

1   Jn. 14.12–14.

very specific circumstances and which, having been created by her, are marked by her forever.

It is important to note that these tendencies are just the flip sides of the same quality of rivalistic thinking. It is as though making the one more unique and the other more ordinary could really help us to understand the completely non-rivalistic benevolence which went into the composer choosing to enter into the drama as a character in the first place. It was, after all, He who opted to be on the same level as all the other characters, making the choice not to be more unique and wonderful than they, but interacting with them so that they should all come to share in his unique wonderfulness in ways entirely proper to them. It was the entire performance that he wanted to infuse with his creative spirit.

At this point, to your relief, I would like to let Rossini go back to heaven – where he belongs – so that he can get on with astounding the angels with different ways of getting them to sing different things, at different rhythms, all at the same time. And I would like to step out of my operatic analogy into its primary analogate, which is of course the living performance known as 'Our Salvation'.

Starting from the End

I want to start from the end, which is of course where we always start from. We can only start from the end because we can only tell stories whose end we already know. We recount them forwards, but we compose them backwards. If we do not know the end, then it is not clear what story we are starting to tell, and thus whether we have a story at all. The end of this story, the drama of our salvation, is the Assumption into Heaven of Our Lady and her Coronation. This is, if you like, the maximum declaration of God's victory in Christ and a sign of the shape of that victory. Of course, the victory was won, the battle was over, the moment that heaven became forever a human story when Christ ascended to the right hand of God, taking a human nature, meaning a lived-out human story, to be the paradigm of heaven. But the fullness of the shape of that victory only really becomes clear with the Assumption into Heaven of Our Lady and her Coronation. That is when it becomes quite luminous not merely that we have been saved, but what it is that has been saved, and what it looks like to be saved.

And what it looks like is this: creation made new and utterly alive. There was somebody who was entirely part of creation, and she was able to participate in the birth of the new creation in such a way that there was no opposition from her to it, no resistance to the bringing about of the new creation, and because of this, there is an uninterrupted continuity between creation and new creation. And this means that creation is good! Everything human is in principle good, and to be brought to a good end. The whole of Mary's bodily life, from Immaculate Conception to Dormition and Assumption, was good. And this means that, in principle, our bodily life is as well. There is nothing intrinsically evil about any part of the human life process, from the fully sexual reproduction by which Mary's parents conceived her, to the moment when her biological finitude reached its proper end in her 'dormition' or death. And so there is nothing intrinsically evil about any part of our human life process – even though in our case the normal strains and stresses of growth and learning get mixed up with our becoming frightened and so grasping onto too small an identity and resisting being taken into the fullness of creation. In that alone, in our being caught up in resisting being brought to the fullness of creation, we are different from Mary.

The difference is between those for whom our involvement in our being created has to reach us first through our being forgiven, so there is a sense of rupture between who we thought we were, where we were trying to head and who we now find ourselves coming to be, and the person for whom there was no such rupture. Her life was the – no doubt stretched and strained – continuous movement towards being created and coming to share in the life of the creator without any resistance or rupture. This does not mean that she did not make mistakes, it does not mean that she did not have to learn, that she found things difficult to understand, that she might have been impetuous, or any other number of character traits. But it does mean that she was – no doubt without any sense of comparing herself with anyone else – fully implicated in the adventure of being given to be who she was to become.

So, from the end of the story, the Assumption and Coronation, we see not only that someone has done something for us, which of course they have; that is Jesus' role, but we also see the beginnings of the living, active shape of what it is like to have that something done for us. But there is more. That the story has come to an end does not mean that it is over and done with, its denizens quietly retired to some celestial Eastbourne. On the contrary, it means that in just the same way as Jesus, the self-giving lamb, is alive on the altar in heaven, his victory having been forever sealed and his self-giving being made alive for us constantly and given to us. In just the same way the sharers in his risen life, the saints – and first among them, Our Lady – are not only part of a story that is now over but share in all the living story-empowering creativity of the resurrection life being made available for us now.

We can put it like this: it is not the case that these are lucky people who are just there on the other side of the great divide, and that we are here, stuck on this side with, in every generation, the same tragic and heroic choices to make, decisions to stick to and so on, which might just get us admitted to the other side, about which we can know nothing. The whole point of the resurrection life being already lived by real people with real names and real life histories, a resurrection life which is cast for us in the shape of the image of creation itself in the Assumed Virgin, is that it means that the great divide is not so great, the other side is even now bending towards us, and tends even to interpenetrate our own side. This means that the adventure is not one of tragic heroism but is a much safer story than we normally dare to believe. After all, salvation that didn't come with an expansive sense of safety wouldn't be worth much.

Making all things new

Now lest you think that in giving you this very highly condensed account of the doctrines of the Assumption and the Immaculate Conception I am merely talking about nice doctrinal symbols, I would like to move back from the end of the story to that mid-point in real lived-out history where we can begin to tell it. And I say 'mid-point' since this story is, as I have mentioned, told from the end. But it is a story which had many dress-rehearsals before it was eventually, definitively and triumphantly performed by Mary of Nazareth. St Luke gives us hints of these dress rehearsals in his use of Greek words which reflect previous attempts at the performance which became definitive in Mary. So the Spirit of God will overshadow (ἐπισκιάσει) her.[2] The dress rehearsals for this include the Ark of the Covenant being overshadowed by the cherubim (συσκιάζοντες),[3] and the Presence overshadowing the Tabernacle (ἐπεσκίαζεν) in the book of Exodus.[4]

But those were the dress rehearsals, and as with all dress rehearsals in some need of fine tuning. For what we learn in St Luke is that the Ark and the Tabernacle were figures of Mary. And not in Luke alone: also in the book of Revelation the Ark is associated with the woman who is to give birth.[5] And this is much more significant than it seems. Because the whole point

---

2   Lk. 1.35.
3   Exod.25.20.
4   Exod. 40.35.
5   Rev. 11.19–12.1.

of the Holy Place in the centre of the Temple, and indeed of the Tabernacle from earlier times, was that it was through the Holy Place that God with his angel hosts made creation. The Holy Place was deemed to be outside created matter and the veil which surrounded it was the beginning of material existence. Moving outwards from the veil there were to be found in the Temple the symbols of the days of creation: the lights, the waters, the animals and so on.

A key moment in the liturgical year would be on the Feast of Atonement, when the High Priest, considered to be a temporary incarnation of the divinity and thus able to be worshipped as YHWH, would come out through the veil, thus symbolizing God coming into the midst of his creation to perform sacrifice for his people. In coming through the veil, he would vest himself with a seamless tunic made of the same material as the veil, thus making the, in principle, Invisible One materially visible. Now St Luke is more than hinting that all these rites were dress rehearsals for the Real Thing. And the Real Thing took the form of the Great High Priest, YHWH himself, vesting himself with flesh to come into materiality and then go up to Jerusalem to perform the real sacrifice. This is the background imagery, if you like, to what is happening at the Annunciation. Mary is to be the real Holy of Holies, the real Ark bearing the covenant, the real Tabernacle into which Moses could not go. And because it is the real high priest, YHWH himself, the Creator, who is to emerge from her, no man needs to go into her first in order to come out again in different robes as would have been the case with the High Priests of the Temple.

I stress this since I think it very important in our post-Freudian era to emphasize that the conception by a Virgin has nothing to do with downplaying sex – a fact underlined by the doctrine of the Immaculate Conception, which makes clear that there is nothing intrinsically problematic about sexual generation. The Virginal conception has everything to do with

Creation out of nothing. And this means that what Mary was being invited to do by the Angel was to allow herself to be the link place, the portal, between the Creator out of nothing and the coming into being of everything that is. That is, she was to be in historical fact what the Holy Place had prefigured. It is certainly beyond my imagination to figure what it must have been like for this woman to find that she was becoming the gateway of creation; that one of the angels which ministered to God before the creation was addressing her, inviting her to become the living portal; that she was to become the incarnation, the permanently contemporary seat of Wisdom, the feminine figure which accompanied God at the creation of all things; that she would in fact become the one our near worship of whom would correct and fulfil the worship of the goddess whose cult was alive in Jerusalem before Josiah's reformation of the First Temple. This is how Luke puts it: 'But she was greatly troubled at the saying, and considered in her mind what sort of greeting this might be.'[6] This is the understatement of the ages!

Of course there is a biological mystery here: where did the necessary extra chromosome come from which alone enables a male child to be conceived? And the only answer I know is a negative one: not from any human paternity, or from within any human structure of desire, parentage, male possessiveness, need to control, or to propagate. Rather it came in the same way that Creation comes: as something out of nothing. But to be fixated on the biological mystery, which seems to have been of little concern to the ancient authors, is to miss the point of what Mary is being asked to live out. She is living out virgin creation, new, fecund, fresh, ripe with constantly birthing possibilities, not run by men, not tied down into property or chattelage. And instead of doing so in the midst of a huge and heavy sacred structure – such as the Temple was – she is doing

---

6   Lk. 1.29.

so as a living human being, who needs protection in her vulnerability, as is shown when Joseph offers her covering from the potential honour killing which could easily have been the lot of an unwed mother.

So, here we have the Holy Place made suddenly alive as the Creator prepares to vest himself with flesh. In the non-canonical *Protoevangelion* of St James, Mary is depicted as being involved in weaving the veil of the Temple when the Angel comes to her for the Annunciation. However historically inaccurate this may be in terms of where Mary was living at the time, it shows at least that the symbolism was well understood: what Mary was doing in the nine months of her pregnancy was in fact weaving the veil of flesh which would enable us to see YHWH come into the world. But it is from *her* flesh that she was weaving, and it is her flesh that is thus inextricably caught up with the making new of all things.

This lived out creative performance by Mary continues when she arises and goes to visit her cousin Elizabeth. When Elizabeth hears her greeting, John the Baptist leaps for joy in her womb.[7] The verb in Greek is ἐσκίρτησεν and it appears in two significant places: it is the same verb which in Hebrew describes David dancing about, skipping, (מְרַקֵּד) before the Ark in 1 Chronicles 15, where also the arrival of the Ark is greeted with great shouts – and the verb ἀναφωνέω is used of the Levites greeting the Ark and of Elizabeth greeting her cousin. Even more significantly, the same Greek word, σκιρτάω (to leap about), puts in its appearance in Malachi 3.20 (4.2) where the gender of the protagonist is normally mistranslated but should be: 'But for you who fear my name, the sun of righteousness shall rise with healing in *her* wings. You shall go forth leaping (σκιρτήσετε) like calves from the stall.'

It is important to notice what has happened in Luke's Gospel: what had been cultic objects, used for occasional

---

7   Lk. 1.44.

symbolic acts, have become fulfilled by someone, Mary, beginning to live out, slowly, painstakingly, in time, what those cultic objects had been pointing to. What Luke is showing is how Creation out of nothing is becoming history, a real performed, lived-out history, over time. And it is this real performed, lived-out history over time, soon to be opened out through her son's protagonism so that we may all become its performers and livers-out, which will itself be the crowning perfection of creation.

Thus we have in Luke's Gospel, as in the others, moments of tension between Mary and Jesus, times when she does not understand, times when she is anxious, times when she has to tuck things away until what they mean can become clearer. And yet this space which includes learning, tension and interaction is the space within which Wisdom, who gives form to creation, allowed Jesus to grow up in Wisdom and in stature.[8] Again it is important to notice that these moments of tension, of misunderstanding and so on are not, as it were, embarrassing lapses in what ought to have been a perfectly uninterrupted motherhood, lapses put in so as to test our faith in the Immaculate Conception. Rather they are parts of the creative tensions of the performance, which was being brought into being by real human beings over time, and by real human beings interacting with each other.

It is the whole of that interactive performance which is made alive for us as something *for us*, as something we can be relieved by, not 'stressed out' by. It means that we can reconsider – to give but one example – that very particular fleshly human reality: the bodily eyes of a mother whose expression over time is moulded by her interaction with her child, being patient when the child is impatient, alarmed when the child is over-confident, tired of the child's mewling and puking, stretched and aged by the whole business of caring at

---

8   Lk. 2.52.

all. There is here all the tension that is proper to Wisdom accompanying creation and making of creation a lived story. And we can consider that it is fully appropriate for us to see all the grace of God available for us through exactly those same time-enriched eyes, which are entirely specific to a woman. Incarnation without living interaction would not be incarnation, and the living interaction then becomes, very properly, part of what the incarnation gives us.

I think this is brought out specifically by John in his treatment of the relationship between Jesus and Mary. In John, Jesus does not talk about 'Our Father' as though he has a Father in common with any other human. He talks about 'My Father' or 'The Father'. It is only at the end of the Gospel, after the Resurrection, that he becomes inclusive in his language, saying to Mary Magdalene: 'Do not hold me, for I have not yet ascended to the Father; but go to my brethren and say to them, I am ascending to my Father and your Father, to my God and your God.'[9] In other words, John seems to be pointing to a sense in which, until Jesus has gone to his death, and then in his Ascension created that new space which is death-lived-in-as-moot-for-humans, the real paternity of his Father couldn't yet be shared in by others. It is in his going to death that he makes available that paternity.

It is also curious that in John's Gospel, although the Evangelist is happy to refer to Mary, Jesus' mother, as 'his mother', Jesus himself never does. When he addresses her, it is in the seemingly formal vocative: 'O woman!' (γύναι). This is the term he uses at the wedding feast at Cana,[10] and from the Cross.[11] And I would like to suggest that, as usual, John is giving us more than seems to be the case. It is as though until Jesus' death, Mary is still in gestation of him and not giving him birth, but that in his dying he gives her, in the person of

---

9   Jn. 20.17.
10   Jn. 2.4.
11   Jn. 19.26.

the beloved disciple, a son, the first of many brothers, and names her *his* mother for the first time. The stretching effect of the interaction between Jesus, Mary, the disciples, and the circumstances of his death is seen as opening up both a new shape to paternity and a new shape to maternity, and this is seen as something creative and deliberate.[12]

What I particularly like about this is that it does seem to make sense of the oddity of the Miracle at Cana. For there, Mary, off her own bat and without anyone asking her to intervene, points out to Jesus that 'they have no wine'. Jesus appears to rebuke her for jumping the gun, as though she is pushing him into doing something before he is ready for it: 'What is there between you and me? My hour has not yet come.'[13] But she is not put off, and tells the servants to do whatever Jesus would tell them, which they duly do. I have long been curious as to why Jesus thought Mary was jumping the gun here, in what is solemnly reported as the first of the signs he worked.

There may be a clue in the book of the prophet Isaiah. As Margaret Barker has pointed out: the Hebrew text of the Qumran manuscript of Isaiah 7.11, the earliest version which we have extant and one contemporary with Christ, reads not, as the (later) Hebrew Masoretic text has it: 'ask a sign of the Lord your God'. Instead there is one different letter: 'ask a sign

---

12 Tina Beattie pointed out to me that some commentators have seen in John's use of 'γύναι' a sign that Jesus is designating his mother as Eve, the original woman. This would mean that from the Cross he is the new Adam designating Mary as the new Eve, the mother of all the living. See also Tina Beattie, *God's Mother, Eve's Advocate* (London: Continuum, 2002) and Tina Beattie, *New Catholic Feminism: Theology and Theory* (London: Routledge, 2006).

13 Jn. 2.4.

from the Mother of the Lord your God'. We may have here a not-yet censored relic from the religion of the first Temple.[14]

This does at least suggest a reason why Jesus should have thought that Mary was jumping the gun. No one had asked her to produce a sign and yet there she was trying to get her Son to produce one. And Jesus' hour had not yet come – which means in John the hour of his death. Might it not be that it is only in his creatively occupying the space of death, when he will bequeath to her the first of many disciples who will call her mother, that she will properly be called 'the Mother of the Lord your God', and thus one who can properly be approached to ask for signs? It is of course typical of the sort of lived performance that I have been talking about that the reality of the abundance and the fullness of what was to be given exceeded its proper place in what the characters imagined to be the script, and came rushing out anyhow, giving even more than the author intended.

There is a point here about the shape of what Jesus was bequeathing to us in his going to his death. He was making available the paternity of God as something which could be shared in by others who were not he, but would be becoming he over time – hence the ease with which he speaks of his 'brethren' after his resurrection. But this paternity was not simply something celestial and removed. It also included being inducted into a family, a living family of faith, with a real woman who is to be mother of all beloved disciples, a motherhood that is a proper part of the making available for us the celestial paternity.

It is this element of family which I would like to bring out. The interactions in the Gospel story show that there was something rumbustious, slightly out of control, about the family relationships being described. And this I think is

---

14   On this, see Margaret Barker, *The Great High Priest* (London: T & T Clark/Continuum, 2003); Margaret Barker, *Temple Theology: An Introduction* (London: SPCK, 2004).

something which is a good and proper part of our life in the Church. No matter how po-faced and sententious, ordered and obedient the dreams of some ecclesiastical males, Mary seems to have a centre of gravity all of her own, one which is not pulled in by, and submissive to, ecclesiastical constructs of what her Son would want. And God persists in gifting us with that tension, that sense of more than one centre of gravity as a relief and a freedom from the consequences of our own monistic, univocal, and frightened visions of what is acceptable.

This I think is worth attending to: the 'mono-' in monotheism can have at least two valencies. One of them is restrictive, zealously hygienic let us say, because God is in rivalry with other gods and needs everything to be narrowed down and made more exact, since the danger of idolatry is everywhere. The other is not in rivalry with anything at all, and is seriously concerned that we will not have enough joy and freedom and happiness unless we are set free from our fear of death and enabled to dare to participate in the life of the Creator. And the more signs of our being loved and encouraged and enabled to belong we can get, the merrier. It is this rumbustiousness of God whose monotheism is decidedly unhygienic, whose oneness is nothing at all like our monisms, trying to get through to us that we are loved, *this* rumbustiousness which means that the shape of the life we are being welcomed into tends to spill over into our world through the prayers and protagonisms of the saints, and chief among them, of course, the portal of the new creation herself, Our Blessed Mother.

So as we begin to consider matters of ethics in the light of Mary's hymn of praise, it is important to remember that non-monistic rumbustiousness whose different centres of gravity save us from our univocal pictures of God, a rumbustiousness which is kept so much better alive when we are dwellers not in ideological cages but in a hugely extended family household of spacious dwelling places, and where the heroism and the struggle for the good which we must learn can never entirely swallow the sensation that we are safe, that we are held, that there are others reaching towards us, that whatever may be the immediate appearances, we are in much more of a playground and much less of a war zone than we are inclined to think. Maybe then we will be making room for *Mary*'s soul to magnify the Lord.[15]

---

15 See also Charlene Spretnak, *Missing Mary* (New York: Palgrave Macmillan 2004); and ARCIC, *Mary, Grace and Hope in Christ – An Agreed Statement* (Harrisburg/London: Morehouse/Continuum, 2005).

2

Living the Magnificat in the Shadow of Globalisation

LINDA HOGAN

At the heart of contemporary economic and social life is a paradox: we live in ever-closer relationships with one another and yet we are increasingly unsure about identifying the values and aspirations that all human beings share. Globalisation through trade, technology and tourism has created an interdependence that touches us all, whether we wish to partake of it or not. Geographical remoteness or cultural isolationism may delay the homogenising trajectory of globalisation but it will not ultimately disrupt it. It is an economic, political and cultural reality. Yet even as this apparently unstoppable integration is in progress, a counter movement, a process of fragmentation is also evident. We can see this in the way we have become ever more fixated on our differences. Politics is endlessly caught up with difference – whether it be of religious affiliation, ethnicity, nationality, gender and sexual orientation – to such an extent that we are increasingly hesitant about referring to categories of shared human experience. Thus even as we become ever more integrated, the mood of late modernity is intensely suspicious of all meta-narratives, whether they come in economic, religious or political guises.

I. Living in a Global Age

That we live in the first genuinely global age is something of which we are deeply aware. This awareness is evidenced by the fact that the language of globalisation and multi-culturalism helps us express the nature of our everyday lives. The usage of these terms is no longer limited to the technical worlds of academia or policy-making; rather they have meaning in the wider social context. Understood as referring 'both to the compression of the world and the intensification of consciousness of the world as a whole',[1] globalisation describes a peculiar interplay of global and local whereby, as Anthony Giddens points out, local happenings are shaped by events occurring many miles away and vice versa.[2] Developments in global capitalism and culture, combined with the phenomenal success of technology, especially in the realm of communications, together create an experience of social and political life that is not only novel, but which is exhilarating for its beneficiaries.

The ethical challenges that are posed by this are manifold. Critics, including those who front the anti-globalization movement, have drawn attention to the negative effects of unregulated or unfairly regulated markets, of the consolidation of economic activity in the developing world and of currency speculation in many parts of the globe. The ever-increasing economic disparity between North and South as well as the shameful impoverishment of the African continent are also seen by many as inevitable but unacceptable by-products of globalisation. In response to this, the former United Nations

---

1   Roland Robertson, *Globalization: Social Theory and Global Culture* (London: Sage, 1992), p. 8.
2   Anthony Giddens, *The Consequences of Modernity* (Cambridge: Polity Press, 1990), p. 64.

High Commissioner for Human Rights, Mary Robinson, has argued for an ethical globalisation that is a form of economic and political integration that is subject to moral and ethical considerations, that respects all human rights, civil, political, economic, social, and cultural.[3] Her point, made in a different way also by Joseph Stiglitz,[4] is that while the processes of globalisation can be beneficial, they are not unambiguously or universally so. Thus we need to create forms of globalisation that serve rather than undermine human development, and this means that the processes of hyper-integration need to be moderated and governed by ethical principles. There is no doubt that the economic imperative of globalisation requires what Brian Hehir calls a humane measuring line by which he means that globalisation in its economic, social, cultural and political dimensions must be evaluated in terms of what it does to the dignity of the person and what it does for the dignity of the person. The dignity of the person in all his or her complexity becomes the critical yardstick in all assessments of the merits, or otherwise, of globalisation.[5]

One of the most controversial and problematic aspects of globalisation is the political and cultural homogenisation that has accompanied, or perhaps that is endemic to it. Works like Barber's *Jihad vs McWorld*[6] and Klein's *No Logo*[7] map the enormous cultural impact of iconic global brands such as Coca-Cola, Nike, and Disney, and identify the many ways in which globalisation's cultural face challenges and often

3   Mary Robinson, 'Human Rights, Ethics and Globalization', Second Global Ethic Lecture, Tubingen University, January 2002, available at www.ireland.com/newspaper/special/2002/robinson/index.htm.

4   Joseph Stiglitz, *Globalization and its Discontents* (New York: W. W. Norton & Co, 2002).

5   Lorna Gold, Brian Hehir and Enda McDonagh, *Ethical Globalization* (Dublin: Veritas, 2005).

6   Benjamin Barber, *Jihad vs McWorld* (New York: Ballantine Books, 1996).

7   Naomi Klein, *No Logo* (London: Flamingo, 2000).

undermines local identities, traditions and social systems. Thus the purveyors of the most unfettered forms of globalisation are accused of advancing Western norms and practices, creating homogenised systems of thought and wiping out local cultures, languages, social structures, and occasionally livelihoods. Yet the paradox is that because of globalisation's effects we are aware as never before of the tremendous richness and diversity of human life as it is lived globally. Moreover most governments and religious leaders are cognisant of the significance and the intensity of this diversity. If one looks closely it is clear that the globalised culture which is alluded to in analyses of globalisation is in fact a multicultural one. Disney makes movies about Pocahontas, and Chinese and Indian food are available almost everywhere. A feature and result of globalisation is a cultural synthesis, which incorporates traditional markers of ethnicity, race or religion from all over the globe. And although the dominant trajectory is still that of Americanisation, it is accompanied by the universal adoption of elements from cultures as diverse as India, Thailand and Argentina. The global presence of the Bollywood film industry, of Thai food and of Argentine tango are indicators of the multicultural nature of this contemporary culture. And although the existence of local ethnic and religious cultures alongside the global one is evident in most states today, the political significance of the consumption of this multicultural global phenomenon are far from clear.

Our global culture is multicultural, but so too are nation states. Thus the difficulties as well as the opportunities associated with cultural, religious and ethnic diversity are concerns for national as well as for global governance. Los Angeles, Paris, Cairo, Johannesburg and Sydney are centres of intense cultural fusion, with people of different religious, racial and ethnic backgrounds sharing the same limited space. Individual and familial immigration over centuries but especially in the late twentieth century accounts for much of this. However, as Will Kymlicka points out, cultural diversity within the state's borders is also often the result of the incorporation of previously self-governing, territorially-concentrated cultures into a larger state.[8] For example, Australia incorporated Aboriginal groups, Canada its first nation peoples, Brazil numerous indigenous tribes, and the USA the American Indians. Moreover, the make-up of modern states as, by and large, composed of many nationalities and polyethnic means that cultural, religious and moral diversity is the context of our immediate experience.

This means that far from being a relentless driver of integration, the empirical evidence suggests that globalisation also sets in train a number of contradictory processes, including a trajectory of fragmentation, seen in the forces of nationalism, identity politics and religious fundamentalism. This ambiguity is signalled by Bauman with his neologism 'glocalization'.[9] Moreover, hidden amid the rhetoric of multiculturalism lurks religion. Although included among the variables that comprise multicultural societies, the political significance of religious differences is frequently undermined. Rarely is the intensely religious character of contemporary contexts, whether local, national or international, fully acknowledged. Yet modern life is saturated with religion. It can be politically engaged or apolitical, 'furious' or irenic, prophetic or domesticated, but whatever its hue the empirical evidence confirms that public life, in its local and global manifestations, is awash with religious voices. Thus it is this paradoxical interplay of local and global, of the particular and the universal, of the religious and the secular that Christians

---

8   Will Kymlicka, *Multicultural Citizenship, A Liberal Theory of Minority Rights* (Oxford: Clarendon Press, 1995), p. 10.

9   Zygmunt Bauman, 'On Glocalization: Or Globalization for Some, Localization for Others' in *Thesis Eleven* 54 (1998), pp. 37–49.

encounter when they ponder the nature of social and political life today.

II. Christian Responses

So how are Christians, both individually and collectively, to respond to this ambiguous legacy of integration alongside fragmentation? What are the questions that should guide our reflection? Is there a distinctive Christian calling in this context? If so, how are we to discern what it is? What resources do we have from our sacred texts and our tradition? Can they have relevance or resonance in a world that is radically different from the contexts of their composition? These questions raise fundamental issues about our under-standing of the nature of morality, the role of individuals within the Church, and the authority of sacred texts and traditions. In fact there are no easy answers to these immense questions. What the Christian tradition gives us is an extra-ordinary inheritance of moral wisdom and teaching from which to discern, both individually and collectively, how to live a just and truthful life today. Of course it is impossible to do justice to this rich and diverse tradition within the limits of one chapter. Consequently, what I propose to do in the remainder of this chapter is to speak first about this legacy in terms of developing a personal sense of virtue and after that to draw out some general themes from different aspects of the tradition that may help us in the broader political context.

Cultivating Personal Responsibility

Christianity operates with a community-based model of ethics rather than with an individualistic one. Moreover it has a vast fund of tradition from which to draw. Most importantly, Christianity regards the words and actions of Jesus, as revealed in Scripture, as inspirational. This means that the Bible is an important source book for Christian moral thinking. Theologians both today and throughout the centuries have held different views on the role which biblical texts should play in Christian ethics. They range from the view that the Bible gives us definite guidance in the form of specific moral laws, to the view that it provides Christians with a distinctive inspirational vision of the virtuous life in the form of values to be cultivated rather than specific, non-flexible rules to be followed. However one conceptualizes this, there is no doubt that the sacred texts of Christianity have a central place in the moral formation of the person. Yet detailed studies of biblical texts over the centuries have shown us that it is extremely difficult to glean from them simple, absolute and universal rules to guide our behaviour. This is because there is a vast corpus of moral teaching in the Bible, some of which is contradictory. Furthermore, some texts like those pertaining to slavery are problematic, while others like the texts on usury have been ignored for centuries in the Church.

It is likewise with the Church's teaching tradition. Of course the moral teachings and traditions of our past should command our attention. However, one of the reasons why the tradition of moral teaching has occasionally been controversial is because we fail to give due attention to the developments and changes that are themselves part of the tradition. We tend to operate with an overly simplistic and unified view of the moral teaching of the Church. We assume that the position now being taught on, for example, slavery, marriage or human rights is essentially the same as, or at least consistent with, what the church taught in the past. Yet when we look at the Church's teaching on human rights this is clearly not the case. When the National Constituent Assembly of France declared in 1789 that 'men are born and remain free and equal in rights' and that 'the aim of every political association is the preservation of the natural and inviolable rights of man,'[10] the Vatican reacted immediately to condemn it. In 1791 Pius VI in his *Quod Aliquantum* claimed that it was anathema for Catholics to accept the Declaration of the Rights of Man and of the Citizen. He insisted that 'this equality, this liberty, so highly exalted by the National Assembly, have then as their only result the overthrow of the Catholic religion.'[11] Yet by 1963 – a mere two centuries later – John XXIII insisted that:

> any human society if it is to be well ordered and productive, must lay down as a foundation this principle, namely that every human being is a person, that is, his nature is endowed with intelligence and free-will. Indeed precisely because he is a person he has rights and obligations flowing directly and simultaneously from his very nature. And as these rights are universal and inviolable so they cannot in any way be surrendered.[12]

This is not simply a conflict between two texts pulling in alternative directions. The tradition has changed, and changed radically. Once the concept of inviolable and natural rights was anathema; today it forms a central plank of the Church's understanding of how the dignity of the person is to be protected and promoted. The nature of the Church's moral

---

10 'Declaration of the Rights of Man and of the Citizen' printed in Hans Küng and Jürgen Moltmann, *The Ethics of World Religions and Human Rights, Concilium* (1990/2) (London: SCM, 1990), pp. 3–5.

11 Quoted in Bernard Plongeron, 'Anathema or Dialogue? Christian Reactions to the Declarations of the Rights of Man in the United States and Europe in the Eighteenth Century' in Alois Müller and Norbert Greinacher (eds.), *The Church and the Rights of Man, Concilium* 12 (1979), pp. 1–16.

12 *Pacem in Terris*, §9 (11 April 1963). At:
http://www.vatican.va/holy_father/john_xxiii/encyclicals/docum
ents/hf_j-xxiii_enc_11041963_pacem_en.html.

doctrine is such that it seems to be able to absorb this kind of radical change and yet retain its authority. And yet we do not immediately or easily think of this kind of flexibility when we speak of the Church's moral doctrine or teaching. This suggests that when we speak about the Church's moral teaching or its moral tradition we should understand it as a living tradition, one that does inevitably change and develop.

Christianity therefore has a highly differentiated sense of the ways in which we learn moral discernment. Centre stage is the Church, which has an important teaching function. Its task is to enable individuals to recognise the moral truth in each situation. It does this in many ways: through moral formation, through the witness of exemplary figures, and through preaching and formal teaching. Each of these forms of moral education is important, although in Catholicism the formal teaching is through magisterial pronouncements, and doctrine tends to be given most attention. To be Christian means that one is always in dialogue with this multi-faceted teaching tradition. One has the security of being part of this community of believers in which one's personal conscience is formed. Thus one's moral discernment is and ought to be shaped by the collective endeavour of the community. So too is it formed in dialogue with the central beliefs of Christianity. It is not therefore an utterly autonomous ethical sense. Rather it is the individual's personal and self-conscious integration of collective moral wisdom with her/his own learned insight.

Often when people ask what resources Christians have to enable them to map their way through the complexities of social and political life they expect a list of rules and regulations giving complete and definitive guidance on specific moral problems. What I have been suggesting here is that if we expect this kind of response then we are likely to be disappointed. We will be disappointed because, as I have argued, our moral inheritance is not an unchanging, timeless and exceptionless tradition but something richer and more expansive than that. So my answer to the question about the resources Christians have to enable them to deal with their social and political contexts is that they are manifold: we have revelatory texts, a rich inheritance of moral wisdom and teaching through the centuries, as well as inspirational stories of moral heroism and exemplary practice. We also have core principles, essential values and virtue together with a community that is committed to guiding individuals in their moral discernment.

Finally it is important to look at some of the insights from this rich and diverse tradition that might guide Christian political responsibility. Here I will draw on the Church's social teaching, as well as on liberation, political, Third World and feminist theologies, in order to identify some core principles to guide our practice. My purpose here is not to draw up an agenda or a framework for Christian social and political thought, but rather to reflect briefly on some of the central principles that seem to me to have special resonance today. The three principles I will focus on are:

1) a new global context for the question, 'who is my neighbour?'
2) human rights as a way to safeguard human dignity;
3) justice balanced with care.

A new global context for the question 'who is my neighbour?'

The turbulent history of Europe in the twentieth century could be read as a collective failure of imagination in responding to the biblical question, 'who is my neighbour?' That history shows us the perils of limiting our concept of neighbour to those who share our religious affiliation or our ethnic or racial group. In fact the metaphor of the neighbour has been highly influential in the Christian moral tradition through the centuries and its potential in the global context is immense. The neighbour is a metaphor that is local and familiar. It resonates with us because it reminds us of our connections to a community as well as to a place, a neighbourhood. Of course these connections are often fragile and difficult. But because they change as our sense of our place in the world develops they can also hold great promise. The metaphor of the neighbour not only reminds us of our connections to communities and places; it also implies responsibility and involves us in reciprocal relationships. Moreover, since these relationships are usually our earliest experiences of relationship outside family, the metaphor taps into a sense of the reciprocal expectations and responsibilities that is deeply familiar to us. For this reason the metaphor of neighbour can nurture a profound moral sensibility and an empathy that is at the core of living ethically.

In the contemporary social and political world, where globalisation is the air we breathe, it is vital that we create an expanded understanding of who the neighbour is. We must now be attentive to the global context for the question, 'who is my neighbour?' This is because globalization through technology, trade, and tourism has radically altered our perception of human life and its diversity. Moreover it has altered our understanding of the intricate and sometimes pernicious ways in which our lives are interconnected. We now know that the choices we make when we visit our local supermarket can have a direct and detrimental effect on a coffee-producing community in Uganda. We cannot help but be aware that many 'safe' forms of medication available in the western world have already been tested on the populations of the developing world in large-scale clinical trials. This global context necessitates an expanded notion of the neighbour, one that can engender a sense of global responsibility and accountability, one that can traverse the now obsolete boundaries of geography, of ethnicity, of religion.

Human rights as a way to safeguard human dignity

At the political level it has become ever more urgent to concretise the respect and care that is due to one's neighbour, understood globally. Since 1948 the language and politics of human rights have become the way to express the rights and reciprocal duties of individuals and governments worldwide. The concept of human rights is based on the central belief that there are some things which all human beings share regardless of their culture, religion, race or gender. It has recently been adopted by the Church as its principal idiom of social teaching. Yet there have been problems with the politics of human rights. Many cultures have protested that their particular perspectives have been obliterated in the name of universal human rights and that one can never completely understand a culture or tradition from the outside. Undoubtedly there are difficulties with the concept and politics of human rights. But these difficulties should not deter us from attempting to articulate our commonalities, from engaging with traditions which are not our own, nor from criticising a specific culture for failing its people in particular ways. Otherwise each individual would be the victim of her or his own culture, without any prospect of external reference.

The human rights tradition articulates a conviction that, regardless of the views of different cultures, individuals do have certain rights. Furthermore, one's claim to have these rights vindicated does not depend on the agreement of a particular government, religious authority or culture. These are rights which the individual possesses by nature and which social and political institutions are duty bound to honour. The dominance of a realist epistemology within Christian ethics meant that the church was well placed philosophically to adopt this thinking. It enabled the development of a specifically Christian account of human rights which may well be another important milestone in the political struggle against injustice worldwide. This Christian account of human rights also has another significant effect in that it has enabled the church to articulate its values in a language that has wider purchase and that resonates globally.

Our understanding of human rights certainly needs to be more historically and culturally sensitive. It needs to take account of the many ways in which power relations infuse academic as well as political discourse. Furthermore, it needs to hear alternative and dissident opinions and to engage with them. Yet, even with all its ambiguities, the concept of human rights represents the best chance we have of protesting against injustice and of protecting human dignity. It contains within it the conviction that the things that human beings share are more fundamental than those things which divide them. It articulates 'the dream of a common language'[13] and the hope that dialogue and mutual engagement will enable us to overcome division. Most importantly, however, it is a universally recognised way of affirming the inherent worth and dignity of each and every human being.

Justice balanced with care

There is no doubt that the rhetoric of social justice is essential. Indeed it functions as a much needed corrective to an earlier tendency within the Church to deal with issues of social justice primarily in a charitable mode. Indeed, at least since the eighteenth century, Christianity has embraced the language and philosophy of social justice and has acted as a significant proponent of social justice worldwide. Moreover this role is all the more notable given the relentless progress of global capital and the related need to address many social and economic issues at a trans-national level. Yet ironically the language of

---

13   This is in fact the title of a collection of poems by the poet Adrienne Rich: *The Dream of a Common Language: Poems 1974–1977* (New York: Norton, 1978).

justice, if used exclusively, does have its limitations. As many feminist writers have pointed out, occasionally the application of standards of strict equality or fairness will not suffice. Indeed this is why within the Christian tradition the demands of justice have tended to be moderated by those of love or charity. Similarly in feminist ethics there has been a recognition that justice needs to be balanced with care, that the conditions for human flourishing are often more substantive than the minimal requirements of justice. It is not that justice loses its central role, but rather that it needs to be enriched by a fuller, more abundant account of social living.

The ethic of care has emerged in feminism to convey a different and in many respects supplementary way of understanding moral relationships and the responsibilities that ensue. The purpose of speaking about an ethic of care is to draw attention to the values of interconnectedness and of relatedness, values that are often ignored in justice-centred discourse. Joan Tronto defines the activity of care thus:

> On the most general level, we suggest that caring be viewed as a species activity that includes everything that we do to maintain, continue, and repair our 'world' so that we can live in it as well as possible. That world includes our bodies, our selves, and our environment, all of which we seek to interweave in a complex, life-sustaining web.[14]

For Tronto, care is an ongoing activity, a practice and a disposition. The ethic of care encourages us to imagine the moral self not as a self-sufficient, utterly independent individual but rather as a self-in-relation. It highlights the ethical significance of contextual, inductive thinking.

---

14 Joan Tronto, *Moral Boundaries: A Political Argument for an Ethic of Care* (New York: Routledge, 1993), p. 103.

Moreover, it values intimacy, engagement, and the maintenance of relationships. Care then operates not as an alternative to justice but rather as an important corrective to its dis-interested, abstract concerns.

There are undoubtedly resources within the Church's own tradition of social thought on which we can draw when trying to unravel the complex demands that the attempts to construct an ethical form of globalisation put upon us today. The fact that, from the beginning, this tradition has preserved the two inter-related discourses of love and justice may suggest a way of proceeding. Indeed the endurance of the twin discourses of love and justice through the centuries indicates that they both have a significant role to play as the Church articulates its own distinctive response to inequality and oppression. Yet to date we have not given much attention to the significance of the presence of these two distinctive modes of social engagement or their inter-relation.

III. Conclusion

A new global context for the question 'who is my neighbour', and human rights as a way to safeguard human dignity and justice balanced with care, are merely contemporary renditions of the values that are already part of the tradition but which have been reinterpreted for this age. Precisely what they will involve in the practical and political sense still needs clarification. Moreover this clarification requires us to work in an interdisciplinary fashion with political, economic and cultural analysts. It is not something that the Church can do by relying exclusively on its own resources. It also involves attending to the nuances and subtleties of different cultural contexts and responding to the particularities of human life in all its diversity. Thus a Christian social ethic is not something that can be accomplished once and for all. We can have no blueprint or prototype, no master plan to be implemented universally. To strive for such unchanging certainties is to misunderstand the nature of the Christian vocation, which is an invitation to live ethically in the midst of ambiguity.

We have many resources for this task, resources that can be gleaned from the rich inheritance of texts, traditions and exemplary practice. However, it is also a work of moral imagination because our knowledge and understanding is always partial and incomplete, our desires are often conflicting and our commitments are often faltering. With this in mind the theologian Sharon Welch cautions Christians to be modest in their hopes. In her book *Sweet Dreams in America: Making Ethics and Spirituality Work*, she suggests that

> rather than hope for eventual victory and for a world without injustice or serious conflict, rather than expect that at some time major social problems will be solved and not replaced by other challenges ... we would be better served by a more modest hope, a hope for resilience, a hope for staying power and effectiveness in the face of ongoing challenges, and a hope for company along the way.[15]

---

15 Sharon Welch, *Sweet Dreams in America: Making Ethics and Spirituality Work* (New York: Routledge, 1999), p. xvi.

3

The Magnificat:
Mary Speaks on Justice

MONGEZI GUMA

T his chapter examines the Magnificat (Luke 1.46–55) and
how, through the voice of Mary, God's message of
transformation is announced. It looks at the Magnificat from
the context of South Africa as we struggle to cope with
challenges of an emerging democracy, forgiveness, and
reconciliation. Many of us within the Anglican Communion
have tended to put a distance between these challenges and
Mary. Some of us have half-heartedly genuflected at Mary in
the fear they may be accused of Mariolatry. As a result we
have deprived ourselves of the opportunity to hear the full
significance of the Magnificat, especially as it talks to the
condition of injustice.

It is perhaps important for us in South Africa to revisit the
Magnificat at a time when we celebrate the fiftieth anniversary
of the historic march of 20,000 women of all races to the then
apartheid government at Union Buildings in Pretoria. That
was a historic moment in which disempowered women said
'no, no more'. Theirs was a heroic endeavour to right the
wrong of the imposition of the hated pass law restrictions, even
to women. It is important that we should allow ourselves to
heed the voice of another woman shouting across the
centuries. At the heart of the Magnificat is an imperative
concerning the role of the Church in social transformation and
the need for redemption of demonic structures and systems
that leave their imprint on the lives of people. The Magnificat
raises crucial questions about how we, as a community,

49

become the embodiment of the promise of a new society; a redeemed people; a transformed community that works for justice, healing and peace. This is coupled with Luke's special message about the responsible use of wealth and possessions. So, in the words of Mary, we hear something about the decisive act of God as He precipitates the reversal of the historic tendencies that invalidate people, and overcomes unjust social relations.

I. The voice of Mary

The voice of Mary, through the Magnificat, reminds us that, even in our day, we have to dismantle the hierarchies of power that confine women to the bottom where they are voiceless and powerless. As an example one simply has to pay attention to the vitriolic response to suggestions that women are ready to succeed the current presidents both in South Africa and the United States. And this resonates with the debate within the Anglican Communion regarding women bishops. It is in just such a world that Mary's Song of Justice has to be heard. As she speaks from her own experience of subjugation and marginalisation, her voice allows for hope for a new world and a new earth. In the Magnificat she invites us to challenge our taken-for-granted world of hierarchies, societies suffering from 'moral catalepsy' and social responsibility fatigue, or what one writer calls 'a Church suffering from tranquil self-delusion'. She invites us to enter into partnership with God in the reordering of the world.

As if to emphasise the special nature of the good news, Matthew introduces his Gospel by telling us about the women who were the great ancestors of Jesus. A closer reading of the names in chapter one – Tana, Rohab, Ruth and Bathsheba – reveals that their common experience was sexual indiscretion. They could be regarded as loose and bad women, 'the sort of people whom others ignore, neglect or despise,' and yet in themselves they are bearers of God's promise.[1] This resembles the manner in which other 'lowly hand-maidens' became the source of information about the resurrection. The disciples are informed by the two 'lowly hand-maidens' that Jesus is risen. Further, the story of the resurrection has to be read through the lens of the Magnificat 'for he has regarded the lowly estate of his hand-maiden'.[2] Here we are connected with a God who cares, a God who makes choices. And the invitation to us is to make the same choices.

Moreover, these passages have to be read against the backdrop of the story of the birth of John the Baptist.[3] Read together, they allow us not only to hear the liberating aspects of the messages but also to appreciate the cultural-religious context of the time that defined and proscribed the role and place of women. Zechariah, as one of the senior priests in the Temple, represents the dominant patriarchal pattern of Jewish culture, religion, and prophecy. The Temple was a symbol of patriarchal space and patriarchal ideological rhetoric and reinscription, with its spatial divisions that reified women's exclusion. At the birth of John, the patriarchal dominance represented by 'name-giving' was silenced. Zechariah's dumbness is the metaphor for the receding old order, and Elizabeth's 'No!' represents the new female vocality in the Kingdom of God.[4]

Mary's and Elizabeth's voices must be heard and understood as breaking the prophetic silence that characterized the

---

1   Mark Allen Powell, *What are They Saying about Luke?* (New York: Paulist Press, 1989), p. 91.

2   Lk. 1.48.

3   Lk. 1.57–67.

4   On this, see Jane Kopas, 'Jesus and Women: Luke's Gospel', in *Theology Today* 43 (1986); Rosalie Ryan, 'The Women from Galilee and Discipleship in Luke', in *Biblical Theology Bulletin*, 15 (1985), pp. 56–59; Elisabeth Tetlow, *Women and Ministry in the New Testament* (New York: Paulist Press, 1980); Elisabeth Schüssler-Fiorenza, *In Memory of Her* (New York: Crossroad, 1987).

centuries before the birth of Jesus. The writer of the letter to the Hebrews says, 'Long ago God spoke to our ancestors many times and in many ways through the prophets. And now in these final days He has spoken to us through His Son.'[5] When in Luke's Gospel we read 'Mary said' (Καὶ εἶπεν Μαριάμ)[6] and Elizabeth's 'No! His name is John' (οὐχί, ἀλλὰ κληθήσεται Ἰωάννης),[7] space is created for new prophetic voices; in a very fundamental way it is a social, cultural and religious reversal of hierarchies of power. What Mary says is both prophetic and eschatological. In what Elizabeth says we hear a public repudiation of religious and cultural pretensions of patriarchy that inevitably leads to women's oppression. The message of Mary and Elizabeth, therefore, is the prolegomenon of that new message of salvation. In a symbolic way the Magnificat is therefore the forerunner of Jesus' 'Programme of Action' that is advertised by Luke: 'The spirit of the Lord is upon me because he has chosen me to bring news to the poor' (4.16–30). There is clearly an affinity between the Magnificat and the Programme.

The other challenge that the Magnificat presents that is linked to renunciation of injustice and oppression is a commitment to the poor and disadvantaged.[8] It talks about a God who does not only favour the rich and powerful but has a place even for those who find themselves languishing on the precarious fringes of our affluent societies. The New Testament scholar William Barclay writes that the word 'poor' is represented by two words:

---

5 Heb. 1.1–2a.

6 Lk. 1.46a

7 Lk. 1.60.

8 On this, see Walter Pilgrim, *Good News to the Poor: Wealth and Poverty in Luke-Acts* (Minneapolis: Augsburg Publishing House, 1981); Luke Timothy Johnson, *Sharing Possessions: Mandate and Symbol of Faith* (Minneapolis: Fortress Press, 1981).

Penes (πένης) – The man for whom life and living is a
struggle, the man who is a reverse of the man who
lives in affluence; and *Ptochoi* (οἱ πτωχοί) – describes
abject poverty in which the person has literally nothing
and stands in imminent danger of real starvation.
These are represented by the oppressed, the abused,
the needy, the humiliated, the despised, and the
marginalized.[9]

This challenges us to do something about the condition of
poverty that bedevils the lives of many. Poverty is deepening
and the gap between rich and poor is increasing. What
exacerbates the situation is an international economic system
'which concentrates wealth ... in the hands of an elite
composed of people of all races, while leaving the majority
poor, if not poorer than before'.[10] For many people in the
south, globalisation has entrenched social and economic
choices that bring about permanent situations of poverty. Such
situations were characterised by the Latin American bishops at
Puebla in 1979 as 'the luxury of the few (that) becomes an
insult to the wretched poverty of the vast masses.'[11] Sadly, in
many instances, the Church goes on as though such poverty
does not exist. While many find themselves, by and large, in
situations of institutionalised injustice characterised by unfair

---

9   William Barclay, *New Testament Words* (London: SCM, 1964), p.
    248.
10 Leslie Milton, 'Be reconciled to God', in Mongezi Guma and Leslie
    Milton (eds), *An African Challenge to the Church in the Twenty-first
    Century* (Cape Town: SACC, 1997), pp. 97–107 (p. 105).
11 Conference of the Latin American Episcopate (CELAM), Puebla
    1979 (§28/128), cited in Leonardo and Clodovis Boff, *Salvation and
    Liberation: In Search of a Balance Between Faith and Politics* (Maryknoll,
    NY: Orbis, 1984), p. 3.

economic, social and political situations and systems, the Church is stuck in theological swamps of respectability.[12]

The bigger challenge is how we could embody an ethos that makes us the Church of the poor. Mary reiterates the prophetic declaration of God's option for the poor. This preferential option is not a rejection of the rich but rather, as Gustavo Gutiérrez, puts it:

> The poor are loved by God simply because they are poor and not because they are morally superior or have a greater spiritual insight, better believers than others; but because it shows the love of God and that the kingdom of God is expressed in manifestations of His justice and love in their favour.[13]

Luke puts in the lips of Mary the challenge for the Church to engage in a ministry that seeks to establish a community of compassion and justice. It is an invitation to the Church to embody a prophetic restlessness that would include a commitment to work for a better and different future. As Mark Powell puts it, 'responsible stewardship includes giving alms (Luke 12.33) remitting debts (Luke 6.27–36), and using one's wealth to promote fellowship (Luke 14.7–24)'.[14] In this the Church would accompany communities in their struggles for survival. Echoing Mary in the Magnificat, the Church would embrace the language of hope that would take the poor beyond the vale of tears. As with Mary, we would be removing the feeling of remoteness of God in the lives of the poor. In this way we would show that God cares for life, and that He

---

12 See also Ernesto Cardenal, *The Gospel in Solentiname* (tr. Donald Walsh, Maryknoll, NY: Orbis Book, 1985).

13 Gustavo Gutiérrez, *The Power of the Poor in History* (tr. Robert R. Barr, Maryknoll, NY: Orbis Books, 1983), p. 128.

14 Powell, *What are They Saying about Luke?*, p. 94.

redeems a humanity obsessed with power and with trampling on the dignity of others.[15]

II. Sophiatown

I serve in the parish of Christ the King in Sophiatown, west of Johannesburg. It was established by the Community of the Resurrection (from Mirfield) in the 1930s. This meant that it was founded in the Anglo-Catholic tradition that drew its inspiration from such luminaries as F. D. Maurice and Charles Gore. The work of the Community of the Resurrection in South Africa was predicated on incarnational theology, or what is sometimes characterized as the theology of 'Real Presence' and Christian socialism. This set the parish on the trajectory of a ministry of justice and confrontation with a government bent on the erosion of the human rights of its black citizens.

In the 1950s Sophiatown was a vibrant and growing community known for its distinctive culture, jazz, the arts and innovative spirit. From 1956 this community was forcibly removed and placed some thirty miles away. Moving people forcibly from their community was a type of cultural, emotional, and physical death. The violence with which people were removed was both direct and indirect. Police with guns and bulldozers demolished houses and those who resisted were arrested. The original community was totally replaced by a white community, and the name of the suburb was changed to Triomf (Triumph). Trevor Huddleston's book *Naught for Your Comfort* captured the story of Sophiatown in all its pain and ugliness.[16] The community was to struggle to 're-invent' itself far away from its original home.

---

15 More generally, see also Earl H. Brill, *The Christian Moral Vision* (New York: Seabury Press, 1979); and Harold T. Lewis, *Christian Social Witness* (Cambridge, MA: Cowley, 2001).

16 Trevor Huddleston, *Naught for your Comfort* (London: Collins, 1956).

In 1997 the new democratic government returned to the Anglican Church the building that it was made to vacate by force in 1962. The Church building is one of three structures that were not demolished from the old Sophiatown. Although it was vandalised inside, with frescos whitewashed and walls broken, the structure represents a link to that vibrant past and stands as a reminder of the inhumanity of the apartheid system. Many of those who are associated with the old Sophiatown – as residents or children of residents – come back to the Church as a spiritual 'wailing wall', and as a way of connecting with this memory. The presence and occupation of the area by those who benefited from their suffering and the inability to reoccupy what were once their homes represent for many a moral challenge and a source of lingering pain. This undoubtedly acts to postpone healing and makes 'reconcilia-tion' difficult. The Church community represents a microcosm of how communities in South Africa are still being confronted by that legacy of dispossession and pain and are struggling with issues of 'closure'. They are struggling to give content to what would constitute healing and reconciliation for them. Furthermore, there is a struggle to search for markers that could serve as a bridge between forgiveness and social justice. However, these struggles and initiatives for 'reconciliation' have to be undertaken against the backdrop of the 'national imperative of reconciliation and nation-building'.

Reconciliation and Nation-building[17]

South Africa, following the first democratic elections in 1994, committed itself to a transition to peace that was not to be characterised by revenge and retribution. As part of the political settlement that brought about the transformation from

---

17 On this see Audrey R. Chapman and Bernard Spong, *Religion and Reconciliation in South Africa* (Pietermaritzburg: Cluster Publication, 2003).

an apartheid state to a democratic one, a commitment was made that while the evil of the past should be undone, evil would not be punished as part of retribution. The biggest casualty of the apartheid state was community and the values that hold it together. The victims were more interested to know the truth of what had happened, and the beneficiaries were more interested in some form of 'amnesty protection'. The country then set in place processes and institutions that were to 'promote national unity and reconciliation'. Among these were first, a government of national unity rather than a majority government. Another was the Truth and Reconciliation Commission (TRC), to concentrate on what was termed 'gross human rights violations', giving amnesty to perpetrators who confessed and reparations to identified victims. A third institution was the Commission for the Restitution of Land, which was to manage the return of land to those who were unfairly dispossessed and to pay restitution to those who could not 'physically return' to their land.[18] These various structures were some of the public means set up to consolidate the transition to reconciliation. The most important symbol of all, however, is Nelson Mandela, who is an embodiment of reconciliation and a paragon of peace-building. It is against this background that the 'people of Sophiatown' had to manage their response to the situation of dispossession from Sophiatown.

Given the national imperative of reconciliation, the people who became part of the Church community in Sophiatown assumed a moral high ground by deliberately seeking to be a 'moral community' in the area. They did not harbour plots of revenge and mass invasions to reoccupy or take over the houses. As I have already emphasised, despite feelings of

---

18 Tinyuko Maluleka, 'Truth, Unity, and National Reconciliation' in Mongezi Guma and Leslie Milton (eds), *An African Challenge to the Church in the Twenty-first Century* (Cape Town: SACC, 1997), pp. 129–33.

'collective pain', national choices had excluded the option of retribution. This moral high ground is best captured in the words of the present Archbishop of Cape Town, the Most Revd Njongo Ndungane:

> We have emerged from a crucible of fire where many people have been wounded and scarred. An urgent task for the Church is the transformation of victims of brokenness into angels of healing.[19]

Of course one has to concede that the notions of forgiveness, reconciliation, and justice are contested terms. There is not space here to tackle the various debates in any detail. Suffice it to say that Trudy Govier,[20] Geneviève Jaques[21] and Maria Ericson[22] among others posit that it is also important to see that reconciliation is ultimately a transcendent matter. Within such an understanding, repentance and remorse are not seen as a precondition for reconciliation. Instead, reconciliation is regarded as a moral imperative and the first locus of transformation is the victim. Talking about what she calls 'unilateral forgiveness', Margaret Holmgren writes:

> The appropriateness of forgiveness has nothing to do with the actions, attitudes, or position of the wrong-doer. Instead it depends on the internal preparation of the person who forgives ... Once this process has been completed, forgiveness is always appropriate ...

---

19 Sermon preached on 30 November 1997.
20 Trudy Govier, *Forgiveness and Revenge* (London: Routledge, 2002).
21 Geneviève Jaques, *Beyond Impunity* (Geneva: WCC Publications, 2000).
22 Maria Ericson, *Reconciliation and the Search for a Shared Moral Landscape* (Oxford: Peter Lang, 2001).

whether the wrongdoer repents and regardless of what he has done or suffered.[23]

Further, as Leslie Milton puts it, '"reconciliation" must be both retrospective and visionary, seeking to heal divisions of the past and to construct a society based on values which the previous system precluded or denied'.[24] He goes on to say:

> an event in the past has affected the total renewal of the relationship between God and the world (2 Cor. 5.19). ... Reconciliation is not simply about how to deal with the past, but about realizing God's promised future.[25]

This challenges us to serve as a bridge between the past, characterised by division and injustice, and a future founded on the principle of equality, human dignity, mutual respect, peaceful co-existence, and humanness (as the 1996 South African Constitution articulates the new vision).

Thus in this instance the emphasis is not on restoration and restitution in order to compensate for past wrongs. Rather, it is on what has been called 'reconciliation and new creation', seeking ways and processes that would contribute towards creating a society grounded on justice.[26] What is described below is an attempt to give a contextual working out of that understanding of healing.

'Pastoral Accompaniment'

The focus in Sophiatown was on 'pastoral accompaniment'. The process was to help many of the Church members come to

---

23 Holmgren, cited in Govier, *Forgiveness and Revenge* , p. 63.

24 Milton, 'Be reconciled to God', p. 98.

25 Milton, 'Be reconciled to God', p. 105.

26 See also Charles Amjadi-Ali, *Islamophobia or Restorative Justice: Tearing the Veil of Ignorance* (Johannesburg: Shereno Printers, 2006).

terms with their traumatic experience, and to journey with them in their personal struggles to effect closures to the inherited hurt. This is predicated on an accompanying optimism about the moral transformation of the wrongdoer. As will be shown below, the hope is that this might be regarded as a 'unilateral initiative' which seeks to ensure a mutual reaching out towards each other.

'Coming back' to Christ the King represents a measure of vindication against the injustice of being forcibly removed from the area. The return and the interment of the ashes of Archbishop Trevor Huddleston in the Sophiatown churchyard was one of the most singular acts of vindication. Huddleston is an iconic figure of the forced removals. His departure in 1956 represented the fall of the last wall of resistance against the removals and draconian laws of the apartheid state.

On return from 'exile' initiatives were started which were intended to redeem the experience of repossession by creating a platform on which the people could not only tell the stories of the old Sophiatown, but also actively to encourage others to collect these stories. Story-telling has been regarded as an important healing tool. In fact, the presumption behind the TRC's public hearings was to give voice, especially to the victims, after those many years during which they were not allowed to cry for their pain and mourn their losses. This process includes collecting memorabilia and 'rubble' from the demolitions that could be excavated. During this process a foundation stone laid by Princess Alice for a clinic in 1933 was recovered. This then makes the victims themselves the custodians of the historical memory of Sophiatown.

The process also includes setting up programmes and liturgical activities of healing. This involves having commemorative services on and around 9 February to remember the first day of the removals in 1955 and also in November to mark the return in 1997. In addition, together with the other churches of Sophiatown collectively referred to as Afrikaans Churches, we have held a Mission to Sophiatown. Participating in this Mission gave us the opportunity to hear and to talk about our mutual fears and anxieties about the situation. This could be seen as what has been called nurturing a 'culture of emancipatory conversations'. The Mission was preceded by conversations between ourselves. These were modelled on the concept of the 'Village of God', where various churches collaborate with one another on various aspects of ministry. It was inspired by Ray Simpson, Guardian of the Community of St Aidan and St Hilda on the Island of Lindisfarne in Northumberland. Unfortunately, we were not able to follow this through with a post-event reflection process, where we could have pursued the issues raised and taken advantage of the rapprochement and reaching out to the Afrikaans community.

The white community, confronted with such a situation, goes through a 'chain belt of emotions'. This includes anger provoked by the presence of the returning community, fear surrounding the uncertainty of what is likely to happen, as well as hesitant participation in initiatives intended to revive the spirit of Sophiatown. Hopefully this will lead to their being increasingly reconciled to the realities around them and allow them to become active participants in the creation of the 'not yet.' In this option of 'reconciliation', there is thus no expectation of public acknowledgement of guilt or complicity in the injustice of the past or of any form of public apology. Instead, there is more an expectation of a willingness to engage in initiatives that seek to create a shared future.

Conclusion

The emphasis of this process is on transforming relationships. The overarching desire is to free present and future generations from the burden of fear and lasting victimhood, hatred and guilt, and a spiral of low key violence. The option taken in this situation could be regarded as 'remedial justice'. At one level there is the 'spiritual and moral accompaniment' of victims, undertaken to help them deal with the scars of oppression and to bring about closure which will hopefully lead to healing. The removal of hostilities has been effected somewhere else. At another level communities have the responsibility to 'negotiate' living together. Although reconciliation does not mean amnesia, the process nevertheless takes up the moral challenge not to be 'conformed to this world, but be transformed by the renewing of your minds, so that you may discern what is the will of God'.[27] In this way we take the moral responsibility in the crucible of life, recognising that decisions in such situations are sometimes ambiguous and messy.

The hope is that a new social reality is established. Mary in the Magnificat reminds us that as people chosen and sent of God, we cannot meet society and deal with its fractures from a pedestal of an assumed moral distance of self righteousness. As has been said, hers is a summons to hope. That hope, expressed in the words of President Mbeki, is this:

> I believe I know as a matter of fact that the great masses of our country everyday pray that the new South Africa that is being born will be a good, a moral, a human and a caring South Africa, which as it matures will progressively guarantee the happiness of all its citizens.[28]

---

27 Rom. 12.2.
28 President Thabo Mbeki, 4th Annual Nelson Mandela Lecture given at the University of Witwatersrand, 29 July 2006, posted at: http://www.info.gov.za/speeches/2006/06073111151005.htm.

4

Hospitality and Holiness

Sr Margaret Magdalen CSMV[1]

Three weeks after arriving in Botswana where I was to live and work in the house of my religious community, the Community of St Mary the Virgin, I was asked to go into the desert with two priests and the Mothers' Union Worker to visit some of the furthest outstations of the Diocese. The Diocese of Botswana covers the whole of the country. Sometimes, at that time, the small villages in the Kalahari got a visit from a priest only once a year – or if transport allowed, possibly twice.

So, the prospect of a visit from two priests, the Mothers' Union worker *and* a Sister was exciting indeed. And in each village we were greeted with overwhelming enthusiasm and joy. But it is from the last of these villages, one that was out on the Namibian border, that I want to share a story.

The people had seen the cloud of sand moving across the expanse of desert long before they could see the actual Land Rover. They were ready to welcome us with singing and swaying, clapping and dancing, and to conduct us to the Catechist's house – which consisted of one room. We sat – and the talking began. The one thing that people in the desert want more than anything else is news – news of the outside world, news of the Church, and news of friends. On this occasion, we had been travelling in the heat of the day for four hours, in hazardous conditions including running into a plague of

---

1   This paper was originally given as a sermon in Durham Cathedral on 8 September 2007, the feast of the Nativity of the Blessed Virgin Mary.

locusts. With nothing more than a cup of tea before we started out, we were hot and thirsty. But it was some two hours before any tea arrived. Botswana was in its seventh year of drought – water was scarce and firewood for heating it even more so. Under those sorts of conditions we were actually being offered exceptional hospitality.

After much conversation, we walked to a school room where we said Evening Prayer and then celebrated the Eucharist. This was followed by a five-hour Mothers' Union meeting at which Anna (the MU Organiser) crammed in as much teaching as possible.

By the time we made our way back to the house I was feeling very empty indeed and looking forward to supper. When it came – eventually – it consisted of a small dish of goat's liver. With African courtesy, a bowl had been brought round to wash our hands and we then began to eat. Other people started to drift in and engage in conversation, and they too were offered food. In Africa, you don't wait to be invited; if there is food, you share it; no-one is excluded. Some while later, I gather, a bowl of rice with spinach was taken to the men who had gone off to continue their talking round the fire, whilst the women made sleeping preparations. They insisted, and would brook no argument, that I slept on the only bed. Next day I discovered that twenty-two other women had slept on the floor crammed in like sardines.

We began the day with another Eucharist – one priest celebrating, the other preaching. There followed a two-hour Mothers' Union meeting, after which we were just beginning to pack the truck when we were called to the Catechist's house once more and offered a cup of tea and a tiny bowl of sour porridge. As we started to eat, one of the priests said to me, 'You know we are eating their famine-relief food?' I was horrified. 'It's all right', he said, 'we have brought them a box of tinned food.' But, that did not alter the fact that they had been prepared to share their meagre and very precious rations with us. I ate all of my porridge as reverently as possible – this was like water from the well of Bethlehem – but I was amazed that all three of the others left at least two-thirds of theirs. It seemed such a terrible waste of the food which had been given so sacrificially.

In the truck going back, Anna said to me, 'Did you notice the children standing at the door as we were eating?' I had indeed seen them wide-eyed and peering in at us, and had rather assumed it was because they had never seen a nun eating before. 'They were there,' said Anna, 'because they would get what we left.'

I could have wept – if only someone had warned me about the cultural thing to do. Why was I so insensitive to the situation? But as a new-comer and a well-fed westerner, I totally misinterpreted the silent pleadings of those children; I was too selfishly wrapped up in my own hunger. To my shame, I came to realise that it was a microcosm of our global situation.

Amongst the many things that I learned in the three countries in which I have lived in Africa, I think the grace of hospitality, and the willingness to share, rank among the highest. One Saturday morning, a boy of about twelve came to our house and asked if he could do any jobs, so we suggested that he might sweep the yard. We always rewarded such work with food – never money. But as it happened we were actually out of food ourselves except for one enormous digestive biscuit left over from a Sunday School party. I gave it to him even though the biscuit seemed so little. He received it with the usual Tswana courtesy. And then, to my astonishment, he went to the gate and called out in a loud voice – from out of the other houses down the street came children running who swarmed around him. I watched as slowly he raised the biscuit above his head in a movement redolent of the elevation at a Eucharist. He then broke the biscuit and gave each child a piece. For me, that was a truly sacramental moment – for

Christ was surely present in that breaking and sharing, in that deeply moving and humbling generosity.

We have a reproduction of Rublev's famous icon in our Convent refectory, and I have to admit that I always thought it was an icon of the Trinity with the three angels sitting around a table, just a small bowl of meat in the centre and a space that invites the viewer to join them. When I discovered the Greek name of the icon was *philoxenia* (φιλοξενία) – meaning 'love of the foreigner', 'welcome of the stranger', or quite simply, 'hospitality', the icon took on a wholly new significance for me. Now, as I look at it, I am always reminded of that other supper table in the Kalahari, bare but for its small dish of goat's liver. 'Do not neglect to show hospitality (φιλοξενία) to strangers',[2] says the writer of Hebrews, and it is immensely humbling to recall vividly the *philoxenia* I received – the love of a foreigner that I was shown – in that far off village in the Kalahari. And I am reminded too of the space preserved for anyone to share it – none excluded. Among desert people hospitality is unquestioning and without calculation.

In his recent book, *Hospitality and Holiness*,[3] Luke Bretherton makes a strong case for hospitality as the *one* authentically Christian way of relating to others, so that in caring for the poor, feeding the hungry, tending the dying and welcoming the stranger, the Christian community finds a way of engaging with others that is true, is transformative of relationships, and effective. It reminds us that, as he accepted hospitality from the lowly, the outcasts and the so-called sinners, Jesus often transformed lives and relationships. And the supper he hosted on that last night, which has been celebrated by the Church in remembrance of him down through the ages, has continued to

---

2   Heb. 13.2.

3   Luke Bretherton, *Hospitality as Holiness: Christian Witness Amid Moral Diversity* (Aldershot: Ashgate, 2006).

have transforming power for all those who receive his hospitality, as we do today at the Eucharist.

But perhaps the greatest of all icons of hospitality is Mary herself whose birthday we honour and celebrate today. For she, quite literally, offered the hospitality of her own flesh where God came to share our humanity. 'Ah, but she didn't offer', you might be thinking. 'He had chosen her. Surely she could do no other?' As one writer once put it:

> Oh, my lady,
> I will not say that God chose you,
> As though you had no option,
> But that God chose to ask you
> And you chose
> To say
> 'Yes'.

Offering that hospitality of her heart was a risk that led to its piercing. 'Her self forgetfulness in accepting God's call was a foreshadowing of the cross. She let go of safety and reputation because of the compelling pressure of God to take up residence in the heart of humanity.'[4] Her response in the Magnificat calls us to a like hospitality of heart, an openness in sharing what we have and who we are without calculation and in ways that involve risk, self forgetfulness and cost.

We *can*, however, rejoice with Mary, for history has shown us that – even in our own lifetime – God *does* put down the mighty from their thrones. Always, without exception, those who use power for their own self-advancement, self-glorification, and self-enrichment, causing untold suffering to God's lowly ones, sooner or later meet with downfall. Tyrants may strut the world's stage for a time but, eventually, all will bite the dust; it is shown so clearly in Psalm 37. God *does*

---

4   Rowan Williams, *Pondering These Things: Praying with Icons of Mary* (Norwich: Canterbury Press, 2002), p. 14.

ultimately cause conceit and pride to crumble; and he *does* exalt the humble and meek:

> not in a role reversal whereby the underdog becomes the upper dog; not by mightily overcoming by superior force all that opposes his goodness and love. Rather he has reversed our ideas of the manifestation and exercise of power.[5]

Amongst the people of the Kalahari who shared not from their excess but out of the very little they had, with such grace, costly generosity and, indeed, delight, I encountered some of the truly humble and meek. And it was through them that I found myself deepened in an awareness as to *why* God bestows favour on his *lowly* ones, *why* he chooses those whose power lies in humility, mercy, justice and love, to be his Christ bearers in the world. I began to learn *why* it is those who are truly hungry and thirsty for him who will be filled with good things – for we cannot know God's mercy if we are already full.

In the Close of Salisbury Cathedral is a sculpture by Elizabeth Frink called 'The Madonna Walking'. It is somewhat ambiguous. Is blessed Mary walking – indeed striding – *away* from the Cathedral that sings her song but does not heed her prophecy? Or is she walking *into the midst of the world* because the celebration of God's mercy in the Cathedral has sent her back to her work? And what is her work? The powerful words of Gerard Manley Hopkins tell us this about her. She 'this one work has to do; let all God's glory through'.[6] Undoubtedly she *will* be that perfect lens of glory, illuminating

5   Mother Jane SLG, *Loving God – Whatever: Through the Year with Sister Jane* (Gwynedd: Cairns Publications and SLG Press, 2006), p. 9 (entry for 15 February).

6   Gerard Manley Hopkins, 'The Blessed Virgin compared to the Air we Breathe'.

our thinking and worship during these few days as we seek to grasp more clearly what it means to live the Magnificat more radically in response to God's cry for mercy, justice and humility.

And one last thought on hospitality and holiness and the possibility of also becoming a lens of God's glory: after our engagement with others through hospitality and sharing, after *philoxenia* to countless people and all the activity involved, we will ultimately be faced with two simple questions: 'Did we see Christ in them? Did they see Christ in us?'[7]

---

7   Adapted from Esther de Waal, *Seeking God: The Way of St Benedict* (Norwich: Canterbury Press, 1999), p. 105.

5

Catholic Openness and the Nature of Christian Politics

MARK D. CHAPMAN

The lure of the Church Party

As part of my monthly spiritual discipline I read *New Directions*, the magazine published for members of Forward in Faith and distributed to many others free of charge – including me. It claims to be a magazine 'serving Evangelicals and Catholics seeking to renew the Church in the historic faith'. It must be said, however, that there isn't much from the Evangelical stable and I doubt if it has very many Evangelical readers. But there is a great deal that emanates from the other end of the ecclesiastical spectrum. It is pretty clear where the magazine stands: the back few pages consist of a directory of 'safe' churches registered with Forward in Faith, many of them under the extended episcopal care of one of the Provincial Episcopal Visitors ('Flying Bishops'), whose diaries appear on the inside back cover. Based on the articles of the August 2006 edition, the main concerns of the twelve men and one woman on the editorial team are to prevent the Church of England going any further down the liberal line, or at the very least protecting the current boundaries of the territory of those who don't want to travel in that particular direction. At the moment in the Church of England this means finding the best possible solution for this very distinct constituency in response to the moves towards women bishops.

Although there is a fair bit of rant in *New Directions*, it must also be said that some of the articles are well written, articulate, and ask very real questions, which organisations like Affirming Catholicism would do well to address. In a clear assessment of the 2006 General Synod debate on women bishops, for instance, Jonathan Baker, Principal of Pusey House asks, 'How should decisions be taken in a divided Church?'[1] Those of us who welcome the idea of women bishops would do well to address that question – the traditional defence of provincial autonomy does not seem to me to be enough. We need to argue in a much more positive and more catholic direction. But that is an issue for another time and place.[2]

What is most fascinating for me in relation to the theme of the present conference is that there is hardly a single sentence in the whole magazine about the world outside the Church – not a word about politics and society, not a word about sending the rich empty away. In fact, the only relief from Church politics in the August 2006 edition comes in the reviews section which features an excellent account of the final recordings of the great Johnny Cash and a review of a book about Ernest Hemingway. I always come away from reading *New Directions* with two thoughts – first, that traditional Anglo-Catholicism is an almost unbearably insular movement which sees itself as under threat from almost all quarters. It is perhaps because of this that it seems to have almost forgotten about the world beyond the Church. Like so much Anglo-Catholicism of the past, contemporary conservative Anglo-Catholicism is principally concerned with protecting its boundaries and with resisting change.[3] It seems to me that this is at the heart of such

---

1   *New Directions*, August 2006, p. 5.

2   See James Rigney, *Women as Bishops* (London: Mowbray, 2007).

3   See W. S. F. Pickering, *Anglo-Catholicism: A Study in Religious Ambiguity* (London: SPCK, 1991), esp. ch. 7.

interesting and novel concepts as the 'See of Ebbsfleet'. And what's more, it's easy to laugh and to sneer at some of the journalism, including the photograph of the bust of Dr Pusey wearing the new house colours of Pusey House red (for the passion of Our Lord, gold (for his resurrection) and black (in mourning for the demise of the Church of England).[4] It is hard to know what Pusey himself would have made of such frivolity.

But *New Directions* also provokes in me a second and rather more troubling thought. Is there not something decidedly Pharasaical in my reading of *New Directions*? Am I giving thanks 'that I am not like these other men'[5] who haven't seen the Affirming light? The truth is, however, that I am always aware that my own strand of Anglican religion can be equally gossipy, insular and as fixated on the internal politics and workings of the Church as that of any Church party. Of course, Affirming Catholicism may be more inclusive and a bit less catty than Forward in Faith, but it sometimes seems to me that some of us have been sucked into affirming little more than the secular values of justice and equality. That may not be bad, but there needs to be more to catholicism than human rights.

Furthermore – which is perhaps even worse – sometimes it seems to me that we have become just another Church party and have begun to define ourselves against other people and groups – if they disagree with us we don't listen to them. But, it seems to me, catholicism needs to be far more than that. If we simply define ourselves negatively then we too will have lost sight of the world-transforming nature of the catholic vision. As that great Anglo-Catholic leader, Charles Gore, first Principal of Pusey House and later bishop successively of Worcester, Birmingham and Oxford, once said: 'We are all

---

4   *New Directions*, August 2006, p. 21.
5   Lk. 18.10.

likely to become embedded in one little clique.'[6] There is, after all, nothing more intolerant than an intolerant liberal – especially as liberals have the necessary truths of reason on their side, which means everybody else must be wrong. It is much too easy for all of us – from whatever quarters – to be seduced into what the American theologian H. Richard Niebuhr called a 'closed society' which 'fills the whole horizon of our experience'.[7] So, I want to ask, how can we resist the temptation to become yet another closed society, a clique fixated on internal Church politics at the expense of what really matters? And what really matters is this: the redemption and transformation of the world, the values of Mary's great song of revolt, the Magnificat.

Catholicism as an open system

By way of a provisional and tentative answer I think we need to begin by looking in a bit more detail at the nature of the catholicism we claim to affirm. To be a catholic Christian is to be able to identify with the historic tradition inherited by the catholic Church – in our case that is the Church of England and her sister churches. And, more importantly, it is to see that tradition as a vital force still capable of transforming our world. The catholic faith is something which was revealed in history. But it is equally true that the faith that was 'once delivered to the saints'[8] is still fundamental in shaping history, in forming our whole approach to society and the world around us – after all, those are the places in which we live our lives and in which we try to follow the path of discipleship. The catholic faith is given in history, but because that history is

---

6   G. L. Prestige, *The Life of Charles Gore* (London: Heinemann, 1933), p. 263.

7   H. Richard Niebuhr, *Radical Monotheism and Western Culture* (Louisville: Westminster/John Knox, 1960), p. 35.

8   Jude 1.3.

not itself complete, because we still await the return of Christ, the catholic faith is always unbounded – it has an inherent openness, and cannot be exhausted by any 'closed system'. Catholicism (and that includes Anglo-Catholicism) is open to the future, open to change, simply because it is orientated to what Rowan Williams called the 'the questioning story of a crucified and resurrected Lord'.[9] For this reason it is still capable of challenge, of disruption, of sending the rich empty away.

The incompleteness of history leads on to what might be called 'apostolic openness and uncertainty'. The Church is the body of those who live in openness, sent to proclaim a message which is always in the process of taking root in new places and new contexts. As the outspoken Scottish Episcopalian Cambridge professor Donald Mackinnon put it: the apostle, the one sent by Christ to make disciples of all the nations,[10] 'is able to teach only so far as he is learning; learning all the time … The ecclesiastic fears it because it robs him of the security which he finds for his own status and mission.'[11] This requires a recognition of the frailty of all human knowing and certainty: 'authority in the present is only effectively exercised in a setting of acknowledged doubt – a doubt to which it may be we are commanded by the imperative of faith itself'.[12] The logic of the Christian faith is a logic of following based on trust rather than certainty – that means following in the path of the disciples and leaving behind the props of the past, the closed systems of Church and nation, in pursuit of worldly transformation. The radical character of the Gospel with its

9   Rowan Williams, 'Does it Make Sense to Speak of pre-Nicene Orthodoxy?' in Rowan Williams (ed.) *The Making of Orthodoxy* (Cambridge: Cambridge University Press, 1989), pp. 1–23 (p. 18).

10   Mt. 28.19.

11   Donald MacKinnon, 'Authority and Freedom' in *The Stripping of the Altars* (London: Fontana, 1969), pp. 51–61 (p. 56).

12   MacKinnon, 'Authority and Freedom', p. 61.

extraordinary demands to follow Christ and Christ alone leads us out of the comfort zone of our closed system to an unknown land – that, surely, is the logic of the first commandment: 'I am the Lord thy God, thou shalt have no other Gods before me.'[13]

In any open system, whether ecclesiastical or political, there will be many unknowns and uncertainties. But so often we pretend that it is not like that. The focus of so much of what we do as a Church is on the visible and the present rather than on the future, with its possibility of transformation. Again it is worth looking at the example of Bishop Gore. He was aware of just how difficult it was to live out the demands of Christian discipleship, especially when one was also a bishop, when one was living as a functionary of what seemed to him to be the closed system of a Church of England hemmed in by status and establishment. Gore was all too aware of just how many compromises were involved in church leadership. He often expressed his exasperation. At Birmingham he once claimed: 'A bishop is a useless creature ... I am going to consecrate a churchyard and open an organ'.[14] The Church seemed fixated on itself, tied into establishment, and almost unaware of the world around it. In a particularly bitter (and famous) reply to the journalist Daniel Lathbury, he remarked: 'the Church of England is an ingeniously devised instrumentality for defeating the objects which it is supposed to promote'.[15] And one might still ask whether a seat in the House of Lords helps or hinders the Church in its task of dethroning the principalities and powers of this world – but that too is a question for another time.

Inward-looking and self-obsessed churches and church parties have often tried to imagine a perfect historical society,

---

13 Exod. 20.3.

14 Prestige, *Gore*, p. 264. See also, Mark D. Chapman, *Bishops, Saints and Politics* (London: T & T Clark, 2007), ch. 9.

15 Prestige, *Gore*, p. 265.

or even an ideal community modelled on the divine relations between the persons of the Trinity. We can easily elevate one little bit of history into our ideal, as we strive to return to this simpler world. There was, for instance, a widespread belief among Victorian architects like G. E. Street and A. W. N. Pugin (as well as many influential churchmen like the Cambridge 'ecclesiologists' J. M. Neale and Benjamin Webb) that the Middle Ages represented the pinnacle of Christian art and theology – and there was a massive project to rebuild churches and society on this model which left only about one hundred English churches untouched.[16] But that sort of historical myth-making can easily be read as little more than the wishful thinking of an increasingly rootless society. And of course the middle ages weren't as they imagined them anyway. The medieval Church's record of crusading, of siding with the rich against the poor, of justifying anti-Semitism in the name of a loving God, simply cannot be ignored. And any other idealised period, whether the 'beauty of holiness' of the Laudian Church of the seventeenth century, the earnest religion of the Tractarians, or even the communist faith of Conrad Noel's Thaxted, is equally problematic.

We like to recreate the past in order to escape the conflicts of the present – we like closed systems, and it is to them that we so often flee. But supposing that there is an ideal church in the past to which we can simply return is sheer fancy – the Church exists and has always existed as a finite human institution. As a historical body it can never be exempt from the struggles of human power; indeed, it has always been the home of conflict. It is perhaps reassuring to know that there is nothing new in our contemporary difficulties. The Church is not some ideal institution into which we escape where we are exempt from the outside world. Instead it is a real body of men and women

---

16 On this see, for instance, James F. White, *The Cambridge Movement* (Cambridge: Cambridge University Press, 1962).

open to all the temptations and ambiguities which characterise human life. It is always immersed in what Donald Mackinnon called the 'grisly complexities and accidents of human history'.[17] Becoming a Christian does not mean that we cease to be human – and most people who have served on Parochial Church Councils or vestries will bear witness to the reality of ecclesiastical conflict.

The trouble with the Church is that it is all too easy for it to become an end in itself and to forget its fundamental purpose – as the late political theorist and theologian David Nicholls put it somewhat contortedly:

> Christians have often replaced a Trinitarian mono-theism by a henotheistic religion which "makes a finite society whether cultural or religious, the object of trust as well as of loyalty" (H. R. Niebuhr). In doing so the Church has transformed itself from being a divinely chosen and guided instrument of God's purpose in the world into an end in itself.[18]

We find it all too easy to create a 'henotheistic' or tribal deity, and when we do so we forget the disturbing presence of a God who lies beyond any finite institution, including our own churches. The Church is not a closed society but one constantly provoked and disrupted by the vision of the Kingdom of God. As Rowan Williams once wrote, at its heart the central story which the Church exists to preserve is founded on 'confrontation with an event, an image of loss, meaning, hope and communication ("*Logos*") rejected by the

---

17 MacKinnon, 'Authority and Freedom', p. 56.
18 David Nicholls, 'Great Expectations: Christian Hope and Marxist Hope' in Kenneth Leech and Rowan Williams (eds), *Essays Catholic and Radical* (London: Bowardean Press, 1983), pp. 278–91 (p. 290).

world'.[19] Of course the image of loss is always balanced by the image of consummation, but we should never forget the limitations of the church as it is. To be an open institution, the Church needs to be able to provoke us to risk all, including perhaps the loss of what we most cherish in that institution we inhabit. We risk all because of the promise of resurrection and hope, but this is something that makes sense only because of the cross.

Anglo-Catholicism and Politics

After this extended preamble on the nature of catholicism, it is now time to move explicitly to the themes of this conference: how does this vision of catholicism as an open system relate to politics? Over the years, many Anglo-Catholics have regarded themselves as 'incarnationalists' – and much of the political tradition of wider Anglicanism has also been incarnational.[20] The reasoning is simple: God's complete identification with humanity, together with the recognition of the goodness of creation, allows Christians to pursue the imperatives of the Gospel through concrete human institutions, which are capable of effecting redemption. However, such an understanding of the incarnation, when untempered by a strong doctrine of sin, has often led to a naive optimism about the role of the

---

19 Rowan Williams, 'What is Catholic Orthodoxy?' in Leech and Williams, pp. 11–25 (p. 19).

20 On the differing traditions of Anglican socialism see E. R. Norman, *Church and Society in England 1770–1970: A Historical Study* (Oxford: Clarendon Press, 1976); Chris Bryant, *Possible Dreams: A Personal History of Christian Socialists* (London: Hodder and Stoughton, 1996); Alan Wilkinson, *Christian Socialism: Scott Holland to Tony Blair* (London: SCM, 1998). For a useful summary of Anglo-Catholic political thought, see Francis Penhale, *Catholics in Crisis* (London: Mowbray, 1986), ch. 8; and John Orens, 'To Thaxted and Back: The Fate of Sacramental Socialism' in *The Anglican Catholic* 17 (2005), pp. 2–19.

state. This tendency is demonstrated by characters like the great nineteenth-century theologian F. D. Maurice, and later in Henry Scott Holland as well as in much of the welfare state tradition deriving from William Temple. God worked his purposes out through a world which was basically good – the institutions of the world, themselves created by God, were as open to his agency as were those of the Church. All that was needed for them to function properly and justly was a bit of gentle nudging in a Christian direction. 'The state,' claimed Maurice, 'is as much a part of God's creation as is the church.'[21] Or as Scott Holland put it: 'The state is a sacred thing'.[22] In turn, the church existed as a witness to that world pointing it to its true centre. In a famous passage Maurice wrote:

> The world contains the elements of which the Church is composed. In the Church, these elements are penetrated by a uniting, reconciling power. The Church is, therefore, human society in its normal state; the World, that same society irregular and abnormal. The world is the Church without God; the Church is the world restored to its relation with God, taken back by him into the state for which he created it.[23]

Even many of the most radical of the Anglo-Catholic socialists

---

21 *The Kingdom of Christ* (1st ed. London: Darton and Clark, 1838), vol. iii, p. 76

22 Charles Gore, cited in Stephen Paget, *Henry Scott Holland* (London: John Murray, 1921), p. 248.

23 *Theological Essays* (3rd edition, London: Macmillan, 1871), p. 403

from Stewart Headlam[24] to Conrad Noel[25] remained deeply influenced by Maurice, despite their use of revolutionary rhetoric. 'Incarnationalism' was frequently interpreted as the gradual deification of nature which meant that the Christian goal was one of reconciliation and harmony brought about relatively gently by the witness of the Church. Society was not a Babylon to be completely overthrown, but was something to be quietly pushed in a Christian direction.

The problem with such an understanding of the incarnation is that it can easily allow us to identify the sovereignty claimed by the state as somehow sanctioned and upheld by God, as if it were beyond criticism. So-called incarnational approaches to political theology frequently fail to offer a liberation from the 'closed systems' of politics. Indeed, it is very easy for us to be seduced by and drawn into these systems. But it is not clear to me that this is really incarnational at all. By colluding with a closed system we can forget the most important political implication of the incarnation: surely what is central to Christ's earthly life is the resistance he demonstrated against the political and ecclesiastical power and authority of his own times.

Things are obviously different today from how they were in Christ's time: there is obviously much that is good in the state and it now gains its legitimacy from a democratic and popular mandate. But however free, democratic or legitimate, still it cannot claim a finality or absoluteness; the state too needs to be seen as an open system. Those in authority are always vulnerable to abuses of power and to neglect their finitude – and here the state resembles the Church. As I argued in my recent book on the politics of New Labour, unfettered power

---

24 On Stewart Headlam, see John Orens, *Stewart Headlam's Radical Anglicanism: The Mass, the Masses, and the Music Hall* (Urbana and Chicago: University of Illinois Press, 2003).

25 On Noel, see my *Liturgy, Socialism and Life: The Legacy of Conrad Noel* (London: Darton, Longman and Todd, 2001).

and state absolutism ought to be constantly questioned and tested, and alternative and more decentralised structures of power and authority have to be developed as a foil to tendencies towards an elective dictatorship.[26] An open, decentralised and critical system should be deeply hostile to the elevation of political systems as if they were beyond question. The logic is simple: 'No relative power, be it that of the nation or its people as well as that of tyrants, can claim absolute sovereignty or total loyalty'.[27] Rowan Williams once wrote (somewhat provocatively) along similar lines in an essay on the political implications of Anglicanism: 'It might even be said that the Anglican Christian has a peculiarly direct reason for adopting a strongly syndicalist view of political power and of the rights of associations over against an encroaching state'.[28] Indeed, it might even be the case that Anglicanism, at least in its disestablished forms, is not intrinsically committed to upholding the pre-established harmonies of the political system at all.

Alongside and often in contrast to the incarnational approach to politics there is another more troubling tradition among Anglo-Catholic political thinkers, called by David Nicholls the 'redemptive' tendency.[29] This pushes political theology in a completely different direction – away from the absolutisation of the state, however benevolent or sweet

---

26 Mark D. Chapman, *Blair's Britain: A Christian Critique* (London: Darton, Longman and Todd, 2005), esp. ch. 7.

27 Niebuhr, *Radical Monotheism and Western Culture*, p. 77.

28 Rowan Williams, 'Liberation Theology and the Anglican Tradition' in Rowan Williams and David Nicholls (eds), *Politics and Theological Identity: Two Anglican Essays* (London: The Jubilee Group, 1984), pp. 7–26 (p. 22).

29 'Two Tendencies in Anglo-Catholic Political Theology' in Williams and Nicholls, *Politics and Theological Identity*, pp. 27–43, here p. 33.

natured or grandmotherly that state might be,[30] towards a far less optimistic picture of the world which sees all states and all political institutions as always open to corruption and the abuse of power. Christ's incarnation was needed not simply to nudge the world in the direction of progress towards the good, but to redeem a fallen world through the political disaster of the cross. There is consequently something utterly scandalous about the doctrine of redemption, which throws into question the securities of the closed system of the rational mind – of which the incarnationalist tendency in Christian politics can be a seductive cipher. For the redemptionists, however, there was something utterly challenging and disruptive about the Gospel of redemption. We might include among their number J. N. Figgis, that neglected Edwardian critic of political sovereignty and monk of Mirfield, as well as the great Frank Weston, Bishop of Zanzibar, and, dare I say it, the current Archbishop of Canterbury.[31] Redemptionists challenged the world and all its systems, political or otherwise – and that meant that the Church could easily risk a complete loss of respectability. As Figgis put it with his usual pungency:

> If we want a Christ amenable to modern notions, a sort of Athenæum Club Gospel, and a Christianity purged of everything that seems abnormal to the critical student at his coffee, our want can never be met. ... It is not to satisfy such that the faith and love

---

30 On 'grandmotherliness' and the state, see David Nicholls, *Deity and Domination* (London: Routledge, 1989), p. 59.
31 See Mark Chapman, *Bishops, Saints and Politics*, chs 4 (on Figgis) and 10 (on Weston). For Rowan Williams and Figgis, see 'Liberation Theology and the Anglican Tradition', pp. 21–3; and his David Nicholls memorial lecture, 'Law, Power and Peace: Christian Perspectives on Sovereignty' (25 September 2005) posted at: http://www.archbishopofcanterbury.org/sermons_speeches/2005/050929.htm.

of Christendom for generations has gone out to 'that strange Man upon the Cross'.[32]

It is the scandal of the cross that allows the Church to elevate itself above the level of mere respectability, and to exist for those who are scandalized by decent society. Thus Figgis wrote:

> It will not be Christ's Kingdom, but something else which will result, if you transform the Church into an institution which might be agreeable for a university extension meeting, but which has no fields where children may play, and is too respectable for the poor.[33]

With such an attitude it was possible to begin to become a Church of the poor through the loss of respectability and status, the 'nervous fear of error when it comes to siding with the poor'.[34] 'Unless we can be the Church of the poor,' Figgis wrote,

> we had far better cease to be a Church at all. ... More and more does it appear that no correctness of dogma, no beauty of Catholic ritual, no sentiment of devotion, no piety esoteric and aloof can secure the Church from collapse, unless she gain a "change of heart" in regard to the relations of wealth and poverty.[35]

---

32 J. N. Figgis, *Antichrist and Other Sermons* (London: Longmans, 1914), pp. 231–2.

33 J. N. Figgis, *The Gospel and Human Needs* (London: Longmans, 1909), pp. 33, 34.

34 J. N. Figgis, *The Fellowship of the Mystery being the Bishop Paddock Lectures delivered at the General Theological Seminary, New York, during Lent 1913* (London: Longmans, 1914), p. 103.

35 J. N. Figgis, *Fellowship*, pp. 99–100.

The Church was the home not of the elect or of the good, but of 'weak and sin-stained souls'.[36] It was the community of sinners struggling to live out their lives of discipleship against an often hostile world. There was nothing easy or harmonious about the Church – it was a rough and difficult place, but, far more importantly, it was also that place where the life of discipleship began.[37]

The politics of openness

All this might be difficult to take when we are so used to the incarnational approach and when churches increasingly become responsible for promoting government policies through community regeneration or by building up what has been called 'faith capital'.[38] And it might seem quite disconnected from my opening remarks on the nature of catholicism as an 'open system'. But there is a connection. We assume the invulnerability of our systems – we idealise our own political institutions. And as we are seduced by the enticements of the liberal political system, so we become reluctant to resist evil and abuses of power within this system – especially where there is an apparent legitimacy and popular mandate. We assume that the institutions of our society embody something of the truth. And of course they do – but only something. Like our Church the state is made up of 'sinned-stained souls'. And because political institutions are never to be equated with the whole truth, Christian political action will always be tentative, resisting power and questioning the assumptions and certainties of the closed systems of the

---

36 J. N. Figgis, *Gospel and Human Needs*, p. 128.

37 On this, see my *Bishops, Saints and Politics*, ch. 9.

38 This term is used in the recent glossy report, *Faithful Cities: A Call for Celebration, Vision and Justice* (London and Peterborough: Church House Publishing and Methodist Publishing House, 2006).

world. To put it less pompously: churches are charged with being pains in the neck for all governments.

The (institutional) Church's role in politics need not necessarily be about influencing governments or gaining a voice in decision-making or representation in the councils of state. There are many good Christians doing that already. Instead there might be a different and far more important role for the catholic Church conceived as an open system: the Church should function to remind political systems of their own need to be open, of their frailty and their lack of finality. The Church as a corporate body will therefore become a thorn in the flesh of any government (although there will inevitably be many Christians involved in that government and taking public office). The role of the Church is to ensure that no political system sees itself as closed, defining itself against other systems and privileging one group at the expense of the other.

Often this means that the Church will simply make the situation far more complex; its theology will often not provide any straightforward answers. Indeed, it is usually when we are beginning to think we have got somewhere and reached closure that we are heading for disaster. As Donald MacKinnon wrote (rather cryptically):

> Can Anglicans learn to receive, not insights simply, but Christian men and women as their teachers of the complexity of the world upon which Christ set the mark of his sovereignty, when alone among the sons of men, himself the Son of Man, he laid all power aside and, at once the man for God and the man for men, on his cross established that place where past bitternesses

86

are not forgotten – no, not forgotten, nor overlooked –
but made new, which is very different?[39]

In the same way that the cross functions as a reminder of
openness, of frailty, of compromise and of complexity in all
human affairs, so in political discourse reference needs to be
constantly made to those places of past bitterness – to those
times when the state has deified itself and set itself up as a false
god against other gods. Just as remembering is at the heart of
our sacramental life,[40] so it should equally be at the heart of
political life, however disturbing that might be for future
cordial relations between church and state.[41]

So let me finish with a call for complexity and openness both
for the state and for the Church. This won't satisfy a tabloid
press or those who clamour for a firm moral leadership. All we
can offer is a vision of a world better than this one but always
glimpsed through the same eyes that are looking at the world
where bitterness is not yet resolved. And maybe the Church
should be the place where we try to live out that complex,
clumsy and painful reality.

---

39 MacKinnon, 'Is ecumenism a power game?' in *The Stripping of the Altars*, pp. 72–82 (pp. 81–2).

40 For a fascinating account of the role of liturgy in the creation of a 'truly, and profoundly, repentant, ex-oppressor-church', see Andrew Shanks, *Faith in Honesty: The Essential Nature of Theology* (Aldershot: Ashgate, 2005), ch. 7, esp. p. 158.

41 On this see my essay, 'Pluralism and Moral Regeneration: Building Community in South African Perspective' in *Journal of Theology for Southern Africa* 119 (July 2004), pp. 4–14.

6

Anglicans around the World

MICHAEL DOE

Stories and Priorities

I want to begin with the good news. I want to dispel the myth that all our fellow Anglicans around the world spend every waking hour worrying about Gene Robinson (the openly gay Bishop of New Hampshire) and planning the demise of the Anglican Communion. My last three years as General Secretary of the mission agency, USPG, paint a very different picture.

Firstly, let me share with you some of the things I've seen on various visits to the places where USPG tries to be the means whereby Anglicans in Britain and Ireland can be in supportive relationships with other Provinces and Dioceses. I think of places like Kuching in Malaysia, where the first SPG missionary made a name for himself working as a teacher, a doctor, and – on his days off – shooting pirates! Today the Anglican Diocese is strong and self-supporting, but when I preached at its 150th Anniversary it was clear how much it still values its USPG connection.

So does the Province of Myanmar – what used to be called Burma. But their situation is very different. Living under a military regime, which has confiscated their schools and hospitals, they look to USPG for ongoing funding and for help with their theological education. I went there to contribute to their first-ever Anglican Gathering, bringing together over two thousand Anglicans, many of them young people. When an army roadblock stopped us four miles away from where they were meeting, they had to come out to meet us, sharing their stories of being the Church in this challenging place.

I think as well of the Delhi Brotherhood, with whom USPG has been in partnership since the beginning, providing shelter for street children as young as four or five, who would otherwise literally sleep on the pavement. And elsewhere in the Church of North India, there is the Bishop of the Andaman and Nicobar Islands, rebuilding his Diocese after the ravages of the 2005 Tsunami.

I think too of the Anglican Church in Tanzania, where USPG channels over £200,000 a year, including support for a new satellite-based internet system which is bringing communication, theological education, and preventative education against HIV and AIDS, to the remotest Dioceses. And elsewhere in Africa, when I went to preach at the Cathedral in Accra in Ghana, I had to wait an hour because they had squeezed in another Eucharist because so many people wanted to make their Communion – that kind of thing never happened to me when I was Bishop of Swindon!

I also think of the Caribbean, where SPG had a somewhat compromised history during the years of the Slave Trade, but where today we are particularly involved in the support of training for ordination. And I think of a recent trip to the Province of Brazil, where on the outskirts of the satellite cities which have grown up around Brasilia, in makeshift camps for homeless people built from wood and plastic sheeting, without sanitation or running water, the Anglican Church is organising social care, Sunday worship and – remarkably – Bible reading groups where people are making the connection between their reality and the Gospel promise of liberation.

I tell you these stories because when you hear the words 'Anglican Communion' I want you to think first about the faithful, and often courageous, witness of our fellow Anglicans around the world. This is the reality of the Communion which we share.

Secondly, I want to assure you that there is, perhaps surprisingly, still a great affection for the Church of England, and for mission agencies like USPG. Of course there are aspects of our history which need acknowledging and redeeming. Of course there is still, in material terms, an element of dependency which mars a real mutuality of giving and receiving. But my experience is that most of the Communion cherishes its roots here: if there is criticism of the Archbishop of Canterbury, it is usually that he has not yet been to see them.

The third thing I want to share from my experience as General Secretary of USPG is that human sexuality – and, for that matter, women in ordained ministry – has never been a central issue. Let me illustrate this from an International Consultation which we recently held in Birmingham. We asked representatives from twenty of the Anglican Provinces with which we are most closely associated to help us discern and plan where USPG should be going. We were humbled by the fact that seventeen came, represented by four Primates – all from the so-called 'global south' – seven senior bishops and four provincial secretaries. We spent the first day by giving each Province the opportunity to share what was important for them in being the Anglican Church in their particular place. No-one mentioned women bishops. No-one mentioned human sexuality. They have more important things to worry about: poverty, HIV and AIDS, being Christian in a Muslim country, being the Church in an increasingly secularist world, and with what's happening to their young people.

Fourthly, my experience is that when our partners do address the issue of human sexuality, there is a surprising range of views, and these do not divide along the supposed North/South lines. For example, here is a view from a bishop from the Indian Ocean who has quite conservative views on human sexuality: 'I will not be labelled, or my views presumed, on the basis of where I live.' Or we can learn from another experience from a Provincial Synod in the global south where I heard the Primate warmly greet the Canadian representative with: 'We may not always agree, but we are brothers and sisters in the Lord, and we will speak the truth together in love'; or again something heard from a bishop in Myanmar: 'It's not our issue. We are just not interested in it'; or from elsewhere in Asia: 'Of course we have homosexual priests here – although here they have to get married – so we're watching with interest how you deal with it in the West.' Another bishop from Central Africa remarked: 'We should be concentrating on our own problems, which are to do with marriage, the way that many husbands treat their wives as subordinate, and the position of women generally.' Another voice from West Africa sums up what many are thinking: 'We don't like what the Americans have done, and we especially don't like the way they've brought it into the life of the Church, but it's their issue, not ours, and we've got more important things to worry about.'

So, to conclude this first section, I am saying all this to dispel the total gloom which seems to have descended over the Anglican Communion. I am aware that for historical reasons USPG is not linked to some of the more conservative provinces like Nigeria and Uganda – indeed, many of the fault lines in the Communion today can be traced back to which mission agency helped found the Anglican Church in each country. I am not denying that in many places there are deep concerns and real risks of schism, and I don't want to sound complacent about some of the real dangers which surround us, but underneath the media headlines, behind the louder, threatening voices, there is much more that is going on.

In all of this USPG is committed to a ministry of mutual support, and, where there are problems, to openness and reconciliation. I regret that some other agencies have chosen to take sides and, if anything, they are making matters worse. What role the Church of England is taking is less than clear. At times it seems to treat the Communion in much the same way that Britain, having lost the Empire, treats the Commonwealth, with a mixture of disinterest and despair. There is, for instance, no world church desk in Church House, Westminster, and no co-ordinated funding mechanisms to support other Provinces. A mission agency like USPG struggles to fulfil our Anglican responsibilities at the same time as many parishes seek alternative self-satisfying projects or opt out altogether. It's interesting that we assume every other Province will state in its foundational statements that it is in communion with the Archbishop of Canterbury, but there is still nothing in our own formularies which says that we are in communion with anyone else at all.

Problems and Divisions

I began with a positive picture of our Communion, but clearly we are also facing huge problems. These arise from the consecration of Gene Robinson in ECUSA, now 'The Episcopal Church' (TEC) (the Anglican Church in the United States) and, to a lesser extent, the reluctance of the Canadian Church to make a categorical refusal of the blessing of same-sex partnerships. Some people believe this was a division waiting to happen – the issues surrounding human sexuality were either the last straw or even what just happened to be first on the agenda at the time. In this second section I attempt some kind of analysis of what has brought us to these difficulties, suggesting that the underlying issue is one of power, often linked to the concept of empire, both old and new.

We may as well start with the British Empire because that's how the Communion began, although at the beginning there was just the Church of England attempting to minister to colonial settlements, and that was often without much thought for the people whose land had been taken over. When I went to Chennai (Madras) to give the opening address at the Synod of the Church of South India, I heard again how the East India Company fought long and hard against any missionary involvement which might moderate its economic expansion. As this book celebrates with Mary the good news of the Magnificat we should remember that in some places the Company forbade its recitation during Evening Prayer lest the idea of 'putting down the mighty from their seat'[1] might be taken too literally!

At the end of the seventeenth century the Bishop of London, under whose jurisdiction these new churches lay, sent Thomas Bray (1656–1730) across the Atlantic Ocean to report on what was happening in the New World. On his return he founded the Society for the Promotion of Christian Knowledge and the Society for the Propagation of the Gospel in Foreign Parts. As the Empire spread, so did the Established Church, and other missionary societies sprang up, each with their own priorities and churchmanship.

Gradually these mission fields became churches and, with some reluctance, the Church of England allowed them to have their own bishops. The Communion itself is relatively recent: in his recent book on Anglican identity,[2] Colin Podmore records how in 1852 SPG celebrated its 150th anniversary in Westminster Abbey, and Archbishop Sumner invited the American episcopate to send a delegation. Probably for the first time the bishops of the United States, and the bishops of the (Episcopal) Church of Scotland, processed together with the bishops of the Church of England, or rather – as it was at the time – the United Church of England and Ireland. Whilst this must have gladdened the hearts of SPG's more High-Church leaders, it was not so acceptable to Evangelicals: many of them still preferred to worship in the Presbyterian – and established – Church of Scotland when going north of the border. A CMS circular of the time continued to refer to the American Church as 'a separate and independent branch of the Church of Christ'.

Fifteen years later in 1867 Archbishop Longley summoned the first Lambeth Conference, and each Conference since has shown the gradual movement to a Communion less reflective of old imperial ties, with perhaps the most significant change

---

1   Lk. 1.52.
2   Colin Podmore, *Aspects of Anglican Identity* (London: Church House Publishing, 2005), p. 22.

coming at the Toronto Congress in 1963 with its declaration that what now binds us together is 'inter-dependence and mutual responsibility within the Body of Christ'.

In recent years the great numerical growth of Anglican Churches in the global south, especially in Africa, has caused some of their leaders to ask why the old colonial power still seems to be in control. In the autumn of 2004 I attended the first-ever All Africa Conference of Bishops. Their theme was 'Africa Come of Age'. It had a strength and confidence which we should welcome, but it is also important to note that North America was represented not by the official Episcopal Church (ECUSA/TEC) but by the conservative groupings such as American Anglican Council and the Anglican Communion Network.

Since then the Anglican Church in Nigeria has decided to remove from their Constitution any reference to Canterbury altogether, and has gone ahead with establishing its own Convocation for Anglicans in North America with a former ECUSA/TEC priest as its first missionary bishop. The Primate of Uganda has denounced the new Presiding Bishop of TEC because of her liberal views – others have rejected her simply because she is a woman. Similarly, once moderate Provinces such as Tanzania have declared themselves out of communion with the supporters of Gene Robinson. Some missiologists call what is happening in Africa 'The New Christendom'. If we were to ask whether the 'global south' is also repeating the mistakes of the old Christendom we might remember that the historical responsibility for both lies as much with us as with anyone.

If we cannot separate our current problems from Britain's imperial past, neither can we separate them from the new imperial power. Today it is the United States that is the new – and now the only – worldwide power. I want to ask two questions about America's role in our current Anglican Communion problems. Firstly, however much TEC may distance itself from the imperial designs of the Bush regime, we still have to ask how far it is still nevertheless tainted by American arrogance and dominance. For despite all its attempts to be sensitive to the rest of the Communion, and to apologise for the consequences of its actions, if not for the actions themselves, there is still a very dangerous assumption in some parts that the success of the 'post-Enlightenment project' is inevitable and it can only be a matter of time before less sophisticated cultures come round to it.

Secondly, we can ask: how far are our Anglican Communion problems the exporting worldwide of divisions within the United States? Just as the eighteenth and nineteenth century British mission agencies exported the divisions within the Church of England around the world, partly to avoid the impact of the Enlightenment back home, we can ask whether we are seeing the current divisions in the American Church being imposed on the Church elsewhere.

This becomes a very important question when we come to analyse what is happening around the whole issue of funding. Western agencies have always used money as a means of controlling the overseas Church, but what we have seen in recent years is a whole barrel of new funding being made available from conservative foundations and leaders of the religious right. This emanates from such bodies as the American Anglican Council, and through some more conservative agencies here in Britain.

This information must of course be treated with care. The fact that one African Primate accepts this funding rather than the (often smaller) sums he used to get from ECUSA/TEC does not mean that he has not already decided that this way lies truth. But money nearly always distorts priorities: there are now very strong funding structures underpinning the relationships between certain African provinces, the new 'alternative' structures within the United States and worldwide, and the right-wing foundations which back them.

It is not difficult to feel that what we are seeing here is part of that larger global picture in which, despite all that is said about postmodernism, the most powerful developments are really what might be called the new fundamentalisms.

What, then, are these new fundamentalisms? First, and perhaps most obvious is economic fundamentalism, the obsession with so-called free trade, so that anything which might obstruct the growth of transnational companies in their control of world trade or their possession of media outlets is to be denounced as evil. Secondly, despite all that the post-Enlightenment theorists have claimed for the triumph of secularism, we see different forms of fundamentalism in religion. Islamic fundamentalism is a subject in itself, but it is the rise of the religious right in Christianity which is splitting the American Church, and which has led to perhaps less than holy alliances with the so-called global south. It has played a large role in the formation of American foreign policy, and, together with the pro-Zionist lobby in the United States, must bear much responsibility for recent events in the Middle East.

I am much taken by Karen Armstrong's analysis of modern fundamentalism[3] – Muslim, Christian and Jewish – that it is not so much a return to pre-modern certainties but rather an Enlightenment-influenced development in which things which were once spiritual and even mysterious have been turned into empirical realities which, like all modern 'facts', must be straightforwardly accepted or rejected.

I would illustrate that by pointing to the way in which 'Scripture' figures in current debates. Pre-modern Christians never treated the Bible in this way. Reformation Anglicans never claimed that everything within the Bible was necessary for salvation. And if you want a telling example of how Scripture is being abused today, look at the issue of divorce: divorce and remarriage are so much part of American Evangelical life that there's no way in which what the Bible so plainly says about it can be allowed to play any part in the current divisions.

---

3   Karen Armstrong, *The Battle for God* (London: HarperCollins, 2000).

We have to ask this question: are we content to let our Christian faith be distorted in this way? Anglicans in the more catholic tradition need to tread carefully here, for we too have a history of claiming complete authority for what we believe, and judging people on whether or not they subscribe to our definitions. Nevertheless – in the name of truth, and in the cause of evangelism – we surely cannot let our Communion be destroyed by something which is so un-Anglican. I might add – also in the name of truth and real evangelism – that there are similar, if softer, dangers in the Church of England, where the catholic tradition is being eased out in the name of a 'mission-shaped church'. As John Hull has pointed out, that can very easily be reduced to a 'church-shaped mission'.[4]

Seeking a way forward

What then are we to do about our Anglican Communion? How are we to deal with this complex and fractious situation? Are we heading for the rocks, and is the vision of one global Anglican family lost for ever? One way forward was set out in *The Windsor Report* in 2004.[5] The Lambeth Commission which produced it was not tasked to look at the issues which divide us – that still needs to be done, despite the fact that the call for a theological study of sexuality was first made at the Lambeth Conference of 1978. Instead it was charged with examining the recent events in North America and their repercussions on the rest of the Communion. It set out the need for what it called 'autonomy-in-communion', which it described as the balanced exercise between the inter-dependence of the thirty-eight Provinces and their legitimate provincial autonomy. It was critical of the way that ECUSA and the Canadian Church had acted without proper concern for the rest of the Communion. Although its criticism of bishops from other Provinces who

---

4   John Hull, *Mission-Shaped Church – A Theological Response* (London: SCM Press, 2006).

5   *The Windsor Report* (London: Anglican Communion Office, 2004).

had subsequently intervened in North America was more muted, it still nevertheless produced a very hostile reaction from those concerned.

The main proposal for a way forward was the creation of a Covenant which all parts of the Communion would agree on and sign, and the Report offered an exemplar text. Most of it is a statement of orthodox belief and practice that most Anglicans would take for granted. There is, in particular, a welcome acknowledgement that 'Communion does not require acceptance by every church of all theological opinion, sacramental devotion, or liturgical practice that is characteristic of the other,' and that 'Every church has the same concern for a conscientious interpretation of scripture in the light of tradition and reason, to be in dialogue with those who dissent from that interpretation, and to heal divisions'.

The sticking point, however, is the introduction of what are to be defined as 'communion issues' and the implication that while up to now we have been held together by 'bonds of affection' and 'instruments of unity' there should now be some way of disciplining those who do not agree with the way that the majority have defined such issues. In his 2006 letter to the Communion on 'The Challenge and Hope of Being an Anglican Today' the Archbishop of Canterbury went so far as to suggest a two tier membership of the Communion: some would be constituent members, other only 'associational', depending on what stance they took on these communion-wide issues.

Many people who identify with Affirming Catholicism have grave doubts about these developments. The way forward which we would seek would begin with a deeper theological reflection on the nature of the Communion rather than the creation of what could become juridical structures. If there is to be a new Covenant it must enshrine and defend Anglican diversity and not provide ammunition for one grouping to bully or even expel another.

So what I would suggest is that in greater accord with our Anglican roots what we really need is to rediscover an understanding of the Church which is not organisational or political but rooted in baptism and (in the widest sense) Communion, that is, not just the eucharist but the communion we have been given, according to the letter to the Ephesians, in Christ. We need an understanding of unity which is based not on uniformity but on hospitality. We need an understanding of authority which is not about imposition but about inter-relatedness. We need an understanding of truth which treasures Scripture, yes, but in the wider context of tradition, reason, experience, and the life of the Church. We need an understanding of Covenant which is not about exclusion, but which enables us to celebrate and struggle with diversity and to carry on travelling together

I believe that a world betrayed by fundamentalisms of various sorts desperately needs a Church which embodies values such as these. What chance is there that our Communion might rediscover them? As divisions widen within TEC, and between North America and most of the rest of the Communion, it is difficult not to believe that these other forces are so strong that those who hold the kind of Anglican values I have described will not prevail. We seem to be facing a wilderness period. In this case our future lies as a righteous remnant – remembering, of course, the danger that a righteous remnant very easily becomes a self-righteous one!

However, as I said at the beginning, there are many Anglicans around the world who are not happy with where we seem to be going; they may have all sorts of questions about many of our Western values; they may have serious reservations about what has happened in ECUSA, Canada, and even the Church of England; but they still have a profound allegiance to the Anglican Communion and a deep commitment to Anglicanism as we have known it.

Finally, then, in the hope that we can find a better way forward, these are three things we could do. First, Affirming

Catholics, and like-minded Anglicans in many other places, need to be much clearer, and much more willing to articulate and defend, the kind of Anglicanism which I have described. And we need to build alliances between such people – for example, between theological institutions which share these perspectives.

Secondly, our agendas, nationally and in the parish, need to concentrate less on smaller ecclesiastical matters and more on the bigger issues, most crucially the issues of justice and peace that the other contributors to this book have been addressing, and which are the pressing concerns for most people here and around the world.

Thirdly, we need to recover the relationships and partnerships which give substance to our claim to being together across the Communion. The report of the Inter-Anglican Theological and Doctrinal Commission rightly said that

> 'thick' ecclesiology, concrete experience of the reconciling and healing work of God in Christ, should take priority over 'thin', abstract and idealised descriptions of the church. Communion 'from below' is real communion – arguably the most vital aspect of *koinonia* with God and neighbour.[6]

Mission agencies like USPG are there to enable this 'thick ecclesiology' to happen right across the Communion, if only dioceses and parishes will turn back from the easier routes of development work on its own or individually-chosen specialist links. We must go on meeting and talking. The next Lambeth Conference, in 2008, needs to happen and all the Provinces need to be invited. And there also need to be lots of other opportunities, perhaps smaller and more personal, creating places where controversial issues can be discussed more

---

6   *Communion Study Report of the Inter-Anglican Theological and Doctrinal Commission* (London: Anglican Communion Office, October 2006), p. 7.

honestly and safely. And perhaps in this way there is hope for the Anglican Communion, and perhaps we shall find that the Anglican Churches here in these islands are also enriched. Please God that it may be so.

7

Who's In and Who's Out?

JOSEPH P. CASSIDY

Getting it wrong

Tonight's Gospel reading[1] has got to be one of my favourites, and I suspect that I am not alone. It's one of those texts that convince us of Jesus' true humanity. I mean, who'd have guessed that Jesus would call someone a dog? Even though Jesus used the diminutive, referring to the 'little' dogs, it's hardly a compliment: in fact, the diminutive almost adds condescension to the insult.

Some commentators suggest that Jesus didn't really intend to insult the woman, that he was sparring with her; but that doesn't take away from the seeming fact that he initially refused to heal this woman's daughter – simply because she wasn't Jewish. Other commentators note that the exclusion is only temporary: the children are to be fed first, which implies that perhaps the outsiders will one day get their turn. But that can be little consolation for this woman and her currently afflicted daughter.

We need to face it: both the saying and the intention behind the saying are jarring, shocking and theologically juicy. The intention and the saying are precisely meant to exclude; and the language used – however you translate it – is a religious, if

---

1 Mk. 7.24–30. This chapter was originally preached as a sermon on 7 September 2006 in Durham Cathedral.

not a racial, slur. Whether mild or harsh, whether said dismissively or maybe even said gently, it is nonetheless a slur.

But what a response from the woman! I know you're not supposed to use the expression *chutzpah* these days, but if I were Jewish and from New York, I'd be forgiven for saying that this woman had real *chutzpah*, in fact *chutzpah* to burn: 'Sir, even the dogs under the table eat the children's crumbs.' What an amazing retort. Or should I say, 'Touché'. She had apparently trumped him. Had there been a debate, the woman's response would have been the sort of once-in-a-lifetime-debate-clincher that you think of, but only hours after the debate has ended.

She parried and won. But Jesus, rather than dreaming up another even more pointed put-down or some face-saving excuse, tells her instead that her daughter has been healed. And that is amazing too.

Many of you will know that this text can be used to argue for radical 'inclusivity' or radical 'inclusiveness' in the Church. The argument goes like this: Jesus had to learn that our inherited ways of figuring out who's in and who's out must be challenged. Indeed, these attitudes can be so ingrained, so habitual, so natural a part of being human, that even Jesus had to have his mind changed by this woman.

Perhaps even more important for contemporary debates, however, Jesus' mind was changed precisely by his attending to his *experience*, to his experience of a Syro-Phoenician woman who seemed to have had a shockingly stubborn faith even though she wasn't supposed to have any faith at all. Jesus might well have presumed that his mission was only to Israel, but there was evidently something about this woman; something that caused him to change his mind; something that caused him to hear God's call in a different way, in a – dare I say it? – more inclusive way.

You can imagine where all this could lead in terms of our assumptions about who should be in and who should be out of the Church, not to mention our contemporary battles in the Anglican Communion. You can imagine too where this leads in terms of appreciating the crucial role of experience, the need always and critically to reflect on and understand our experience. And we *should* feel the powerful challenge of this text, even if it does not, even if it cannot, even if it must not, automatically lead to any simple 'therefores' – the simple sort of therefores that cut off debate rather than foster it.

That said, if Jesus heard his Father through this persistent woman, if Jesus could have got such important things wrong, couldn't we, couldn't we as the Church today, have got other things – other very important things – similarly wrong? If Jesus was persuaded by this stranger, shouldn't we all be open to being persuaded by one another?

The Changing Good

I'm going to change gears; for this text has an important jewel hidden in it. The jewel is the realisation that we must sometimes change our minds on ethical issues because the good keeps changing on us. I know that sounds horrible. I appreciate that it sounds as though I'm going to champion a form of relativism that seems to draw everyone's ire these days. But I'm afraid the good really does change, and I'm also afraid that those who cling to what used to be good may end up inadvertently hurting themselves and others.

Even though Luke tells us that Jesus grew in wisdom and in favour with God (Lk. 2.52), the tradition tells us that he remained sinless. But how could Jesus get away with calling someone a dog – I mean that's got to be a baby sin or a venial sin at least! If you're not sure, try excluding someone from something by calling them a dog, or even just a little dog, and see what reaction you get.

But there's a way through this: there's an important insight that allows us to hang on to Jesus' sinlessness while allowing

105

him to use at least such exclusive if not such offensive language. And the insight is the hidden jewel I mentioned before. The insight is realising that the moral good is not set in stone. The moral good – what I really and truly ought to do – changes in time, across cultures, within religions, even within a communion of autonomous local churches, and not necessarily at the same rate or in the same way everywhere.

The point is this: God does not, God cannot, require us to be ahead of ourselves, to know what is unknowable, to do the good that is as yet unimaginable. We're not built that way. And the universe isn't pre-built that way. We learn in time, through centuries, through millennia; we inevitably learn some things the hard way, by getting things wrong and realising our mistakes – just as Jesus must have done. And as we learn, the moral good – that is, what I ought to do – actually shifts.

The perennial challenge is to do our very best to identify and to choose the best moral option actually available to us. But we can't do what we can't possibly imagine doing. That's the key point. We make all our choices with humility, with some very real fear and trembling, as we choose with all the limitations that are implied in our being human: we're not omniscient; we're not infinitely wise; we can't foresee the effects of all our decisions; we're blinded by emotions and by our inherited ways of understanding and misunderstanding our world – yes, even by our inherited religious, cultural and racial biases. But God nonetheless wants us to choose as best we can, knowing only too well that we'll end up short of the ideal. That's God's will for us. God has willed us to be fallible (and that's true both before and after a primordial Fall). Being fallible is an inevitable part of being human – even if you're the fully-human Son of God.

A few examples may help. Quite a few Roman Catholic ethicists will argue that before we had adequate prisons capital punishment might actually have been morally defensible. Today, however, when we have alternative ways of protecting the innocent from those who would murder, it is no longer defensible. Capital punishment might truly have been the most reasonable, the most responsible, thing to do in the past. If you follow the argument it might even have been God's will – but it no longer is. I know that sounds jarring, but it really does follow if we believe that we were made less than God, as limited, quite fallible beings. We are 'loved' fallible beings, to be sure, but fallible beings nonetheless.

Here is another example: it might have been reasonable to treat one's slaves with compassion; but once we realised that slavery was wrong, the question then became moot. God no longer requires us to treat our slaves properly. Now we ought not to have slaves at all. Or take another example: it might have been wrong to practise artificial means of birth control when we thought that procreation was the primary, overriding aim of marriage; but once we shifted our view of marriage, then it was no longer obviously wrong – at least for some of us. A final example is this: prior to the development of the polio vaccine, there was no moral obligation to make it available to anyone. A new good was yet to emerge. Now a new moral obligation exists.

I cite these examples to suggest that, before we learn that calling people dogs might not be acceptable, we don't have any real moral culpability for doing so. But once the penny drops, then a new moral possibility and a new moral obligation emerges – one that never existed before. Jesus' actual sinlessness is reflected more in the seeming fact that he 'got it in one', than in an unwarranted presumption that he could never have said anything like that.

The key to all these examples is to realise that new moral options emerge – sometimes because we have different structures, sometimes because we make new discoveries, sometimes because we understand things differently. It has always been that way. And that's certainly not relativism; no, this is simply the realisation that the good, what you and I really ought to do, is always concrete. It must always be do-able. Some ethical principles may remain always and everywhere the same (like love your neighbour); but the concrete good often changes (how actually to love your neighbour). The good changes for us, and it changed for Jesus too.

That should not surprise us. The moral good does not pre-exist out there somewhere, waiting to be discovered; that's a form of Platonism, I'm afraid. Rather the concrete good changes as new possibilities emerge. God's expectations change as we change, as our world changes. The real moral challenge is not just to do the 'eternally-preordained right thing', but to set up the conditions, the structures, so that new and better things become imaginable, become conceivable, and so become do-able. This is the key to the common good tradition, the justice tradition, which was so strong in twentieth century Roman Catholic social teaching.

I apologise if this feels like a lecture rather than a sermon, but I think it allows us to make some sense of the challenge of the justice theme of this conference. For the real challenge is not just to sit back and figure out which choices ought to be made in a given situation. Of course we need to do that. But the bigger challenge is to figure out how we change the situation, change our structures, change our hearts, so that we all have better choices – so that we desire the Kingdom that can come. Just think of past elections: weren't there times when you didn't like any of the options? Weren't you – to a certain extent at least – morally incapacitated by the lack of real choice? The most significant moral challenge is to ensure that new moral possibilities (sometimes new candidates) emerge.

Jesus' encounter with the Syro-Phoenician woman changed Jesus' options. Once Jesus recognised her real faith, his calling her a dog was no longer an option. His horizon changed; his range of options shifted. A new good emerged as a new possibility. The challenge for all of us Christians is not simply to develop some calculus to enable us to choose the right good, but rather to dream of what could be; to have our horizons shifted; to have our assumptions undermined by the unexpected grace discovered in another person, especially the stranger. The challenge is to be open to the kind of reversals reflected in the Magnificat (the guiding text for this Conference), where the proud are scattered, the mighty put down, the lowly exalted, the hungry filled, and the rich sent empty away.

Most importantly, this is a challenge not just to those with whom we disagree, but to ourselves as well. What is crucial is that we are open to encountering the Syro-Phoenician women of this world; we need to have the humility to ponder the grace we unexpectedly and inexplicably discover in others, the grace active in those whom we're secretly tempted to call 'dogs', or even just 'little dogs'.

8

Justice and Joy:
Participating in the Mission of God

STEPHEN COTTRELL

I begin with something seen on a tee-shirt in Reading: 'Galileo was wrong: I am the centre of the universe!' The astonishing conceit of this claim stopped me dead in my tracks: 'Ah,' I thought, 'a sermon illustration!' Not only was this declaration a penetrating insight into the soul of our culture, it was also a window on the soul itself, or at least that twenty-first century manifestation of an age old issue – human self-centredness. For we do indeed imagine ourselves to be the centre, and the consumer culture in which we dwell offers ample opportunity for delusions to be massaged.[1]

Ours is an age which has tried hard to dispense with God. We don't need that pathetic prop anymore. We have also stopped believing that politics can deliver progress. All the big promises of previous ages seem to have fizzled out. But we still crave something. There is nothing left to do but re-set the compass of the universe to self. I am the brightest star in the galaxy. Everything else revolves around me in dependent and adoring orbit.

---

1 Much of what follows in the first part of this chapter is adapted from my forthcoming book *Do Nothing to Change Your Life: Discovering What Happens When You Stop*, to be published by Church House Publishing.

We still need and want other people – in fact we need and want them more than ever for they provide the affirmation we crave – it's just that they don't exist in their own right as equal players in a drama whose centre is elsewhere. They are satellites upon which we can shine. The narrative which now makes sense of life, and around which other things revolve, is 'my life'. Anything which happened before is of little value, for it was only a prelude to the real story which begins with me. And is there anything afterwards? Well, we don't think about this one, for the end of our life is truly the end of everything.

In order to bolster this conceit it becomes ever more necessary to disconnect with anything that might put us back in touch with the essential, independent otherness of other things or other people. We end up only caring for other people when their lives affect us. And we stop caring about people whose lives do not touch ours – as if they don't exist at all. And all the problems of the world – from teenage pregnancies to melting ice caps, AIDS, animal testing, Third World debt, fair-trade, race hatred and religious intolerance – are all entirely inconsequential for they don't affect me. Hence there is little interest in wider issues of justice and peace unless they directly impinge on our lives. 'I am not pregnant; the water levels are not rising in my town; I don't have AIDS; no one has ever harassed me because of my race or colour; and no one has ever experimented on my pet cat, so why worry?' This is the attitude of self love, and we learn it early.

Occasionally one of these issues will rise up and affect us. Then we set about changing the world on this one thing. As W. B. Yeats commented in his dark poem 'The Second Coming':

The best lack all conviction
While the worst are full of passionate intensity.[2]

We fail to make the connection between the things that affect us and all the other things with which we generally collude that hold back the flourishing of the world. Politics, we say, like religion, has only caused the world's problems and can't solve anything.

But even as we say this, the foundation of our worldview slips a bit. In order to keep ourselves at the centre, and in order to stave off the end of the universe – which is, of course, the end of our life – much must be done to foster inner peace and outward beauty. From the smorgasbord of new age spiritualities a perfect creed of tranquil self-delusion is constructed where crystals, herbs and incantations dull the pain of impending self-demise. And creams and potions, designer labels, surgery, botox, collagen injections, rhinoplasty, and harsh regimes of exercise and diet battle with the body's steady decay.

Even here we can spot a hideous paradox in the culture itself. We are expected to put self at the centre and worship self advancement, yet at the same time we are endlessly bombarded with images of how we *ought* to look and how our lifestyles *ought* to be. We can only draw the conclusion that somehow being yourself isn't good enough. Indeed it is impossible to switch on the television or open a magazine without seeing some youthful vision of sexually charged and highly toned humanity. With it comes the empty promise that this car, or that perfume, or this diet, or that surgical operation will deliver the body/salary/sexual fulfilment we crave. And none of it does. Or to be more accurate: it delivers just enough

---

2   W. B. Yeats, 'The Second Coming' in *The Collected Poems of W. B. Yeats* (London: Macmillan & Co, 1933).

to get us hooked. We wear the tee-shirt, but its insistence that 'I am the centre of the universe' now appears rather desperate; for the inner truth is that we don't feel this way at all. We pretend it is what we want, and we desire it with the same despairing hunger of any junkie, but in order to get it we now realise that what we really want is to be someone else. Our own pathetic imitation of humanity is too fat, too old, too ugly, too poor, too ordinary (too human, too frail). Actually, we hate ourselves. That is what believing yourself to be the centre has achieved: nothing at the centre except a self-loathing and a futile desperation to be someone else – someone rich, someone beautiful.

Magnificat and Mission

From this horrible malaise there is only one cure I know. It is to put something else at the centre. But how and where will we find such a thing?

And then we hear Mary's song – at least I long for the Church to find a way of singing Mary's song so that it can be heard in the world. It is a song of hope and justice, a song about the re-ordering of creation. 'My soul proclaims the greatness of the Lord' (Lk. 1.46) – that is, God is at the centre and my soul sings for joy to know my God. Mary's song is therefore the song of mission: God's mission of love in which God's Church participates. For we Christians only have one thing to share: and that is to share what we have received from God in Christ. As has been well expressed in the *Mission-Shaped Church* report: 'It is not the Church of God that has a mission in the world, but the God of mission who has a church in the world.'[3] Mary has received this missionary vocation

---

3   Archbishops' Council, *Mission-Shaped Church: Church Planting and Fresh Expressions of Church in a Changing Context* (London: Church House Publishing, 2004), p. 85.

through the blessing that she has received from God and through the reordering of her life. She is now able to give from the overflow of what she has received. She participates in the mission of God and she sings of God's priorities for the world. God's mission is vast and beautiful. From the safeguarding of the biodiversity of the planet to the salvation of every human soul, God has a concern for human wellbeing in its tiniest detail and its every aspect.

God sees the sadness, the confusion, the injustices, the vanities of the world, and he reaches out to us in love through Christ. We are invited to put something else at the centre of life, and then allow the whole of life to be reordered. This is what it means to be an Apostolic Church. This is the hope that the Christian church offers to the world. We place ourselves in the 'sending' flow of his love. This is also the highest – indeed, the only – motivation for mission. We long to see the world as God sees it. We long to re-order the world around the revelation of God's loving purposes revealed in Christ, who is our centre.

To know this is to live the Magnificat. For the first person to find this way of living was Mary. Quite literally, Christ comes to occupy her centre. It is hardly surprising that her first reaction was one of dumbfounded disbelief – she cries out: 'How can this be, since I am a virgin?' (Lk. 1.34). Nevertheless the message of the angel is the message that God offers to every human person who seeks to align their will with the will of God: 'The Holy Spirit will come upon you ... the child that is born in you will be holy, will be called Son of God' (Lk. 1.35). Just as Jesus was conceived in the womb of Mary the Virgin, so Jesus can be conceived in the centre of our lives, in our hearts and minds. God will remove the heart of stone that loves only self and give instead a heart of flesh; a heart like Christ. Then we can love the world so much that it can be changed. Consequently, to participate in the mission of God is a matter of justice and of joy.

115

It is the subject of Mary's song. She sings of God's loving purposes. She is the lowly one whom God has lifted high. She is *Theotokos*, God bearer, and the invitation of the Christian life is the sharing of this vocation. And it is a topsy-turvy proclamation: the proud routed; princes and governors pulled from their thrones; the rich turned away and the poor, the lonely, the broken, the unlovable and untouchable, and all those on the edge, brought to the centre. It is a vision of barriers broken down, hierarchies overturned, a new humanity revealed and re-created in and around Christ.

The Promise of the Magnificat

This brings me on to the subject of a certain cathedral that had better remain nameless. Earlier this year I was leading a training day for the clergy of the Diocese of Durham and having set them some group work to do, I went for a stroll around the building. Standing behind the rope which kept me out of the chancel, and looking at the beautiful reredos behind the high altar, I read this sign: 'Beyond this barrier is the Sanctuary – the Cathedral's Holy of Holies.' And I was dismayed. Now I know signs like this can be found in cathedrals up and down these isles, but the incongruity of this one hit me with real force: had whoever wrote it never read the New Testament? Has Mary's song not been sung at Evensong day after day, century after century? 'He has brought down the powerful from their thrones' – and, we might add, priests from behind their altars – 'and lifted up the lowly' (Lk. 1.52).

Indeed, in St Mark's account of the passion, as Jesus dies on the cross, the veil of the temple is torn in two (Mk. 15.38). This is a hugely significant moment in the story of salvation, for the veil in the temple represents the separation between God's presence in the Holy of Holies, and our presence outside it. As Jesus dies, this veil is rent asunder. This is what Christ does for us on the cross. A new relationship with God is established – a New Testament. From now on God is not located and

116

constrained or impressed by certain religious practices, or to be found only in certain places. Neither is his spirit limited to certain people. And there is also here another wonderful Gospel paradox. We put Christ at the centre of our lives and discover that he has put us at the centre of his. As St Paul proclaims: 'Do you not know that you are God's temple and that God's spirit dwells in you?' (1 Cor. 3.16).

This is the promise and the hope of the Christian faith. This is the 'sure and steadfast anchor for the soul' of the Letter to the Hebrews. And hear this all you lovers of barriers in churches and cathedrals, and all other wearers of the infamous tee-shirt! It is 'a hope that enters the inner shrine behind the curtain' – and therefore removing all the barriers – 'where Jesus, a forerunner on our behalf, has entered, having become our high priest forever' (Heb. 6.19–20). This is the end of story. The Old Covenant is dispensed with. From henceforth the religion shop is closed and we can never fool ourselves again that God is interested or persuaded by our rituals or our glowing self-assessments. All have been found wanting. And in Christ all have been redeemed. He is the one through whom, and around whom, a new humanity is established. This is a community of love, which is nothing less than the community of God, revealed to us as Father, Son and Spirit, and whose company we are invited to share.

This means that when we speak about the Holy of Holies we are speaking about the place where God dwells, *which is in us* – the holy people of God, a chosen race, a royal priesthood, a holy nation.[4] Paul expresses this re-ordering of creation and the new humanity in the most astonishing terms: 'As many of you as were baptised into Christ have clothed yourselves with Christ. There is no longer Jew or Greek, there is no longer slave or free; there is no longer male and female; for all of you are one in Christ Jesus' (Gal. 3.27–28).

---

4   See 1 Pet. 2.9.

It is taking the Church a long while to understand the significance of this text. It took about ten or fifteen years to begin to understand what it meant that in Christ there is no Jew, no Greek. That was the first great challenge to the Christian faith. Was it necessary for Greek converts to receive the sign of the first covenant before they received the second? The conclusion of the early Church's meditation on this question opened the way for the missionary expansion of God's Church. In Christ, racial, cultural and religious identity is no longer the deciding factor.

It took a further 1,800 years for the Church to get its head round the fact that in Christ there is no slave nor free. And at last, in the nineteenth century, slavery began to be abolished, because in Christ social identity is no longer the deciding factor.

And of course – I hardly need point this out at a Conference of Affirming Catholicism or, for that matter, any meeting of anyone in the Anglican Communion – we are still working out what it means for sexual identity no longer to hold such sway; for in Christ there is no male or female. These words of St Paul do not mean that these distinctions no longer exist, but that they are subordinate to the new reality, which is God's kingdom where all are first born sons and daughters, and where the forgiveness, acceptance and love that we find in Christ place everything else in a new perspective.

God is always turning things around, pulling down and raising up. The pattern of the Gospel is therefore always one of poverty receiving glory, of isolation drawn into community. Mary not only tells this story; she embodies it through the alignment of her will to the will of God: 'Let it be with me according to your word' (Lk. 1.38). As Max Thurian has written:

Mary, the first Christian Woman, is also the first revolutionary of the new order. The Church, of which

118

the Virgin is the type, cannot proclaim the good news
of salvation without at the same time making the love
of God concrete in the defence of justice for the poor
and needy.[5]

From henceforth all generations will call this woman holy; and
all generations who hear her song and follow her son must
make the concerns of God's their own. Otherwise God's
mission is reduced to spiritual self-help, or worse, a sort of
scalp-hunting for Jesus, where the very barriers he came to
break down are re-erected in his name and we play the same
old religious game of counting some in and excluding others.

If our motivation is to see the world as God sees it, and to
see each person as God sees them – regardless of race, caste,
class or kin – then our desire to see people come to know Jesus
as their Lord will be inseparable from our desire to see God's
kingdom established, but we will be more able to keep humble,
knowing it is God's mission, not ours.

And what are God's concerns for the world today? God
longs to reach out to the stranger in our midst, to the alien and
the orphan. God longs for us to learn how to live with each
other and to accept one another in the same way that we have
been accepted by Christ. God cries out for the rain forest that
we pillage; for the animals we exploit; for the seas we plunder;
for the ozone layer we destroy.

And in this country, how can we even begin to make poverty
history when we are contemplating spending billions of
pounds – 25 billion being the latest estimate – for the
redevelopment and manufacture of the Trident Nuclear
weapons programme. We embarked upon a very expensive
war looking for weapons of mass destruction. But where are
the weapons of mass destruction? Well, I can tell you where

---

5   Max Thurian, *Mary, Mother of the Lord, Figure of the Church* (1963)
(repr.; London: Mowbray, 1985), p. 93.

those weapons are: they are on British submarines based at Faslane, and they are developing new ones at Aldermaston, just around the corner from where I live.

God wants to turn upside down the priorities of our world. And God wants to do all this through his Church, his people – that community of men and women who are gathered around Christ – an eccentric Church, people who have their centre outside themselves. We are a missional community, our evangelising expressed through our proclamation of God's kingdom. Therefore, despite the fears and injustices that stalk our world, I want to sing for joy from this platform at this conference. Brothers and sisters it is God's justice and God's re-ordering of creation that Mary proclaimed, and because in Christ we are the inheritors of such a hope, then our participation in the mission of God is a thing of great joy.

It is great joy because as well as being good news for the world it is good news for me! I am the one for whom Christ died. I am the one where his Spirit longs to dwell. I am part of his new creation and I can find the affirmation, the joy, the hope that I long for when I invite Jesus Christ to dwell in my heart. 'Oh come to my heart, Lord Jesus, there is room in my heart for thee'. I am invited to participate in the life of God and it is from this sweet communion that the life of mission flows.

Seeing the world through God's eyes, and seeing myself through God's eyes, will also enable me to see how my life must change. Most of all I will discover how much I am cherished and loved. I will discover my belovedness. I will find what it means to be myself in Christ.

While the world tells me that being myself is not good enough and bids me become a faithful and dedicated consumer in order to become someone else, the Gospel invites me to become the person I was always meant to be, the person I can become when Christ is revealed in me. W. H. Auden put it like this in what must be one of the greatest religious poems of the twentieth century:

> The blessed will not care what angle they are regarded
>   from,
> Having nothing to hide.[6]

This transparency of life before God and before each other is the gift of faith. Perhaps we recoil from allowing ourselves to be seen in this way, and from enjoying such intimacy with God, because in our hearts and minds the barriers are still in place. Perhaps we still wear the tee-shirt underneath our other clothes, preferring no God at all, or one made in our image, or a relationship where God is kept in his proper place.

But this is the whole point of the Christian faith. In Christ God has turned things around. With the shocking irresponsibility of love, God has abandoned his station and knocking the barriers down, he has come over to our side and shown us how to be human. This is God's gift to God's world.

When I glimpse this; when I receive this as the astonishing, unmerited good news of God's love for me and all the world, then I cannot help but sing for joy. For our God is a tombstone roller, barrier buster, barricades breaker God who will not be confined or constrained by our definitions, and is leading us towards a new humanity.

> He has come to the help of Israel his servant,
> mindful of his faithful love. (Lk. 1.54 NJB)

---

6   W.H. Auden, 'In Praise of Limestone', in *Collected Shorter Poems* (London: Faber and Faber Ltd, 1966), p. 241.

Index